Interactions 2

Writing

4th Edition

Cheryl Pavlik
Margaret Keenan Segal
With contributions by Laurie Blass

McGraw-Hill/Contemporary

A Division of The ***McGraw-Hill*** *Companies*

Interactions 2 Writing, 4th Edition

Published by McGraw-Hill/Contemporary, a business unit of The McGraw-Hill Companies, Inc., 1221 Avenue of the Americas, New York, NY 10020.

This book is printed on recycled, acid-free paper containing 10% postconsumer waste.

3 4 5 6 7 8 9 0 QPD/QPD 0 9 8 7 6 5 4 3 2

ISBN 0–07–246909–9
ISBN 0–07–112390–3 (ISE)

Editorial director: *Tina B. Carver*
Series editor: *Annie Sullivan*
Developmental editor: *Nancy Jordan*
Director of marketing and sales: *Thomas P. Dare*
Project manager: *Rose Koos*
Senior production supervisor: *Sandy Ludovissy*
Coordinators of freelance design: *David W. Hash/Michelle Meerdink*
Interior designer: *Michael Warrell, Design Solutions*
Senior photo research coordinator: *Carrie K. Burger*
Photo research: *Pam Carley/Sound Reach*
Supplement coordinator: *Genevieve Kelley*
Compositor: *David Corona Design*
Typeface: *10.5/12 Times Roman*
Printer: *Quebecor World Dubuque, IA*

Photo Credits

Chapter 1 Opener: © Ulrike Welsch/Photo Researchers; p. 2: © David Young Wolff/PhotoEdit; p. 5: © Jeff Greenberg/Photo Researchers, Inc.; p. 6: © Deni McIntyre; p. 12: © Tom McCarthy/PhotoEdit; Chapter 2 Opener: © Spencer Grant/PhotoEdit; p. 29 *(top)*: Barbara Rios/Photo Researchers, Inc.; *(bottom)*: © Sean Sprague/Stock, Boston; p. 24 *(left)*: © Renate Hiller/Monkmeyer Press; *(right)*: © Felicia Martinez/PhotoEdit; p. 26: © Bill Anderson/Monkmeyer Press; p. 32: © Katrina Thomas/Photo Researchers, Inc.; p. 33: © Robert A. Isaacs/Photo Researchers, Inc.; Chapter 3 Opener: © CORBIS; p. 38: © CORBIS; p. 42 *(left)*: Michael Newman/PhotoEdit; *(right)*: Ogust/The Image Works; p. 50: John Fung; Chapter 4 Opener: © Robert Brenner/PhotoEdit; p. 63: © Michael S. Yamashit/CORBIS; p. 67: © Nita Winter/The Image Works; Chapter 5 Opener: © Bill Bachmann/PhotoEdit; Chapter 6 Opener: © Associated Press/AP; p. 84 *(top)*: AP/Wide World Photos; *(middle left)*: © Michael Newman/PhotoEdit; *(middle right)*: © David Austin/Stock, Boston; *(bottom)*: © Lucos/The Image Works; p. 90: © Burbank/The Image Works; Chapter 7 Opener: © Michael Newman/PhotoEdit; p. 96: © Mary Kate Denny/PhotoEdit; p. 100: © Gale Zucker/Stock, Boston; p. 103: © John Fung; p. 105: © Barbara Alper/Stock, Boston; p. 106: © Spencer Grant/PhotoEdit; Chapter 8 Opener: © John Wald/Stock Boston; p. 112: John Fung; p. 121 *(left)*: © Mark Richards/PhotoEdit; p. 121 *(right)*: © John Fung; Chapter 9 Opener: PhotoDisc; p. 129: NASA; p. 132: © StockTrek/PhotoDisc; p. 137, p. 141: NASA; Chapter 10 Opener: © Michael Weisbrot and Family Photography/Stock Boston; p. 146 *(left)*: © Culver Pictures, Inc.; *(right)*: © L. Mangino/The Image Works; *(bottom)*: © John Thoeming; p. 149: © Joel Gordon; Chapter 11 Opener: © Dick Blume/The Image Works; p. 160 *(left)*: © Steve Skloot/Photo Researchers; *(right)*: Paul Miller/Oakland Tribune/Sygma; p. 161: © Charles Harbut/Archive; p. 163: © Dennis MacDonald/PhotoEdit; p. 169: © Mulvehill/The Image Works; Chapter 12 Opener: © Skjold/PhotoEdit; p. 174 *(top)*: © Bodhan Hymewych/Stock, Boston; *(bottom)*: © John Fung; p. 175: © Harriet Gaids/The Image Works; p. 180: © Susan Wook Wagner/Photo Researchers, Inc.

INTERNATIONAL EDITION ISBN 0–07–112390–3

www.mhcontemporary.com/interactionsmosaic

Interactions 2

Writing

Interactions 2 **Writing**

Boost your students' academic success!

Interactions Mosaic, 4th edition is the newly revised five-level, four-skill comprehensive ESL/EFL series designed to prepare students for academic content. The themes are integrated across proficiency levels and the levels are articulated across skill strands. The series combines communicative activities with skill-building exercises to boost students' academic success.

Interactions Mosaic, 4th edition features

- updated content
- five videos of authentic news broadcasts
- expansion opportunities through the Website
- new audio programs for the listening/speaking and reading books
- an appealing fresh design
- user-friendly instructor's manuals with placement tests and chapter quizzes

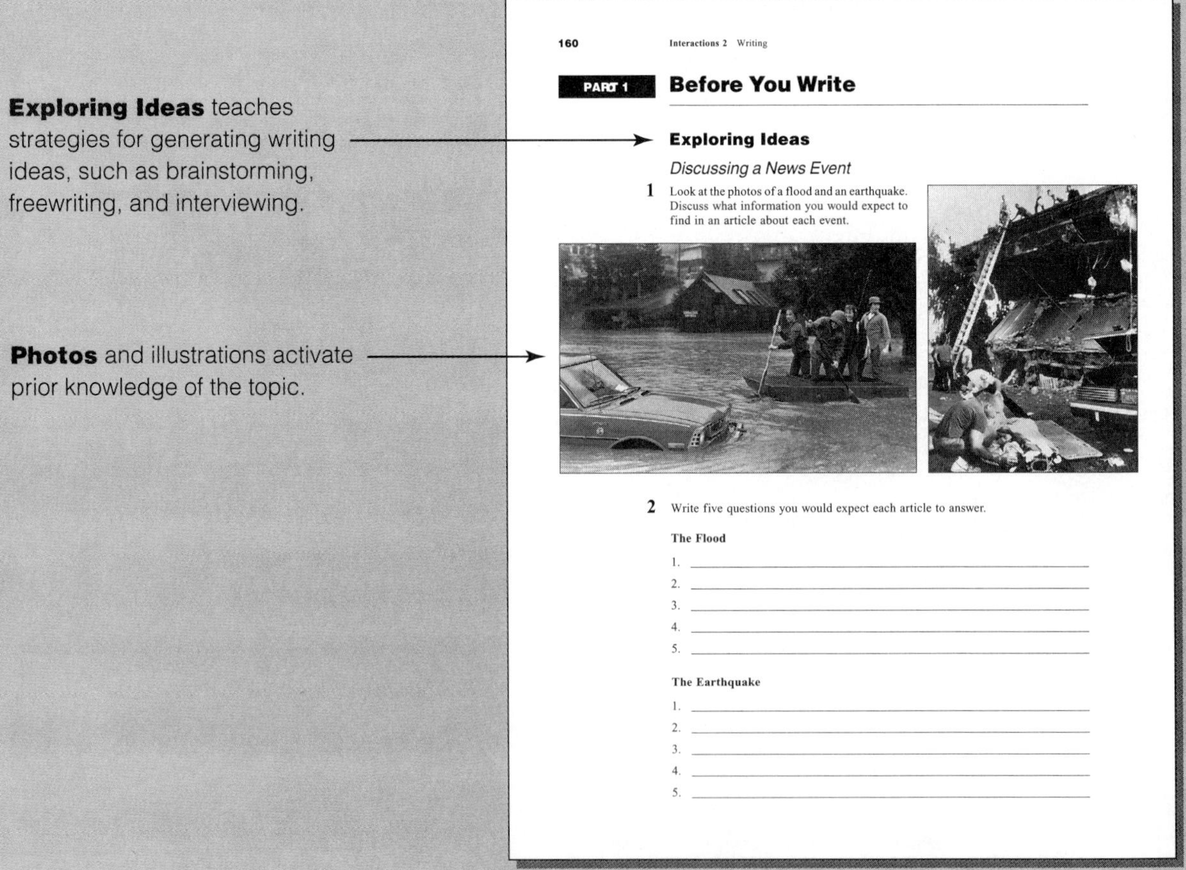

160 Interactions 2 Writing

PART 1 **Before You Write**

Exploring Ideas

Discussing a News Event

1 Look at the photos of a flood and an earthquake. Discuss what information you would expect to find in an article about each event.

2 Write five questions you would expect each article to answer.

The Flood

1. ______
2. ______
3. ______
4. ______
5. ______

The Earthquake

1. ______
2. ______
3. ______
4. ______
5. ______

162 Interactions 2 Writing

Building Vocabulary

4 Add to this list any new vocabulary or expressions from your discussion and questions.

Nouns	Verbs	Adjectives	Other
blaze	break out	burned	overcome by smoke
fire company	injure	burning	
firefighters	rescue	heroic	
firetruck	save	hospitalized	
flames		dramatic	
inferno		courageous	
(the) injured			
smoke			
victim			

5 Complete the chart with the word forms. Use a dictionary to help you.

Verb	Noun	Adjective
injure	______________	
rescue	______________	
	______________	courageous
	______________	hospitalized
	______________	heroic

Organizing Ideas

Answering Questions in an Article About an Ev

The first paragraph of an article gives you the most important answers these questions, sometimes called the five Ws.

Who? What? Where? When? Wh

6 Read the following article. Then underline the words that answer questions.

Vocabulary Building activities introduce language students may use in their writing, and develop strategies for learning vocabulary.

Organizing Ideas develops organizational skills such as outlining, writing topic sentences, and limiting the information in a paragraph.

88 Interactions 2 Writing

Focus on Testing

Diagramming Your Ideas

In Organizing Ideas, you practiced clustering. This, and other kinds of diagrams can help you save time when you are writing under pressure. Take a few minutes *before* you start writing in a testing situation to diagram your ideas. You can draw a cluster, or any other kind of diagram, such as a flow chart, that works for you. This will help you organize your ideas and see how they are related before you write.

Timed Activity: 8 Minutes

Give yourself five minutes to draw a diagram listing the effects of cars on modern life. After you are finished, compare your work with your classmates' work. Are there any important ideas that you left out?

PART 2 **Write**

Developing Cohesion and Style

Choosing the Correct Part of Speech

When you write a paragraph or longer composition, be careful to use the correct forms of words that have different forms for different parts of speech.

Examples

I have an appointment for a medical *examination* today.
The doctor *examined* the young boy.
The medical *examiner* said that the man had died from a heart attack.

1 Complete each sentence with the correct part of speech of the word in parentheses.

1. Many countries are worried about increasing ______________ (immigrate) and have strict laws to control the number of people who can become citizens.
2. ______________ (tourist) is an important source of revenue for a lot of countries.

Focus on Testing prepares students to succeed on standardized tests.

Developing Cohesion and Style focuses on transition words, connectors, and grammatical structures that unify a paragraph.

34 Interactions 2 Writing

4 Edit this paragraph for form. Look for two run-on sentences, three misspelled words, four tense errors.

> My family live in a new neighborhood a few of miles from the center of a large city. Most of my neighbors came from the country. They leave their homes and families to get better jobs and more opportunities for their children. Because they used to live on farms, they like to live with nature. Plants cover every bit of their small front yards. Most of the houses are small, many of them are not finished yet. The houses are made of cement. Even though they are still building, they try to make their houses pretty, they paint them bright colors such as orange, purple and turquoise. Most of the families are working hard to earn money to finish their homes. The people in my neighborhood are very friendly and helpful to each other. In some ways, we are like immigrants in our own country.

Editing Your Writing

5 Edit your first draft using the following checklist. First, check your paragraph for content, organization, cohesion and style, using items 1, 2, and 3 in the checklist. Then edit your paragraph for grammar and form, using items 4 and 5.

Editing Checklist

1. Content
   a. Did you add enough descriptive details?
   b. Did you use a variety of adjectives?
2. Organization
   a. Is your topic sentence the main idea of your paragraph?
   b. Do all the details develop the topic sentence?
   c. Did you include a concluding sentence?
3. Cohesion and Style
   a. Have you given reasons for your feelings?
   b. Have you varied the word order of your sentences?
4. Grammar
   a. Did you avoid run-on sentences?
   b. Did you use correct verb forms?
5. Form
   a. Did you use correct paragraph format? (indentation, di words between syllables, margins)
   b. Did you use correct punctuation? (capitalization, comm
   c. Did you check the spelling of words you were not sure

Editing practice allows students to apply what they have learned by editing a paragraph containing common errors.

Editing checklists equip students with a variety of tools for editing their work thoroughly.

Chapter 6 Global Connections 93

Peer Editing

3 Exchange papers with another classmate and edit each other's paragraphs. Circle or underline in pencil any words, phrases, or sentences that you don't understand or that you think need to be corrected. Then return your paragraphs. Discuss any questions you have with your partner.

Writing the Second Draft

4 Rewrite your paragraph neatly, using good handwriting and correct form. Then give it to your teacher for comments.

PART 4 A Step Beyond

Expansion Activities

1 Find an article in a magazine or a newspaper that talks about the global village. Does the writer mention any effects that you and your classmates have not thought of?

2 Interview classmates and/or teachers about the global village. Compile their reactions and write a composition incorporating their opinions.

3 Interview an older friend or relative about how his/her world has changed in the past 30–40 years. Take notes. Then, in small groups, share your findings with other classmates.

4 Have you ever heard of a time capsule? A time capsule is a group of items that can tell people in the future something about the way people live today. Some people put such items in a box or other container, close the container, and put it away. They write instructions telling people not to open it for 100 years or more. Work in small groups. Brainstorm a list of items to put in a time capsule. They should be items that will best help people in the future understand what life is like now. Brainstorm a list of items. Then discuss them and choose *only* ten items for your capsule. When you finish, join another group and share your lists. How are your items similar? How are they different? Why did you choose these items?

Journal Writing

5 Write about one or both of the following topics.

1. Write about how you think your world will change in the next twenty years. Write for fifteen minutes.
2. Write about any aspect of the global village that interests you.

Peer editing promotes collaboration while giving students valuable editing practice.

Expansion activities encourage students to activate their writing skills in new contexts.

Journal Writing activities promote personal expression through writing.

126 Interactions 2 Writing

Video Activities: The Coffee Lover

Before You Watch. Discuss the following questions in a group.

1. Do you like to drink coffee? Why?
2. How would you feel if you drank ten cups of coffee every day?
3. As far as you know, does coffee cause health problems for some people?

Watch. Discuss the following questions with your classmates.

1. How many cups of coffee does Kat drink each day?
2. Does she plan to stop drinking coffee?

Watch Again. Read the statements below. Decide if they are true (T) or false (F). Then watch the video again to check your answers.

1. ____ Kat has worked in the same place for 45 years.
2. ____ Kat doesn't drink coffee in the evening.
3. ____ Scientists now believe that coffee raises cholesterol levels.
4. ____ If you drink too much coffee, it can make your hands shake.
5. ____ If your heart is weak, drinking coffee will make it stronger.

After You Watch. Interview a classmate using the questions below. Fill in your own answers too.

Questions	Classmate's answer	Your answer
a. What is your favorite drink: coffee, tea, or something else?		
b. How many times a day do you drink it?		
c. How do you drink it (with milk or sugar, hot or cold, etc.)?		
d. Do you think you will ever stop drinking it?		

Use the information in the chart to write a paragraph about you and your classmate's favorite drink(s). Begin with a general statement about your similarity or difference. For example, "Both Charlie and I love to drink tea." Then use expressions of comparison and contrast in your sentences (for example, *both/neither, while, in contrast, on the other hand*).

Video news broadcasts immerse students in authentic language, complete with scaffolding and follow-up activities to reinforce writing skills.

Don't forget to check out the new ***Interactions Mosaic*** Website at www.mhcontemporary.com/interactionsmosaic.

- Traditional practice and interactive activities
- Links to student and teacher resources
- Cultural activities
- Focus on Testing
- Activities from the Website are also provided on CD-ROM

Grammar	Editing Skills	Critical Thinking	Test-taking Skills	Video Topics
■ Giving reasons: *Because, so, therefore* ■ Transition words: *In addition, also, first of all, finally* ■ Making general statements ■ Avoiding overgeneralizations	■ Paragraph format ■ Editing for correct use of present tense	■ Ranking arguments	■ The importance of transition words	■ An Online English Class
■ Giving reasons: *Since* ■ Varying word order in sentences	■ Correcting run-on sentences ■ Editing with the topic sentence in mind	■ Classifying sense details	■ Brainstorming for ideas	■ Garbage Car
■ Modals *must, have to, should, ought to* ■ Stating opinions: strong and moderate	■ Avoiding faulty reasoning ■ Correcting spelling errors ■ Correcting syllabification errors	■ Evaluating arguments for faulty reasoning	■ Supporting your opinion	■ A Teenage Stockbroker
■ Past vs. present perfect tense ■ Present perfect vs. present perfect continuous tense ■ Demonstratives	■ Omitting unimportant details ■ Using correct capitalization ■ Using correct verb forms	■ Implying qualities	■ Checking for correct tense	■ I Love My Job
■ Past perfect tense	■ Omitting digressions ■ Using correct verb tenses	■ Analyzing the moral of a story	■ Checking for chronological order	■ Telecommuting
■ Choosing the correct part of speech ■ Restrictive relative clauses	■ Punctuating relative clauses	■ Defining terms	■ Diagramming ideas	■ Teen Talk

(continued on next page)

Grammar	Editing Skills	Critical Thinking	Test-taking Skills	Video Topics
■ Verbal adjectives (*surprised/ surprising*) ■ Gerunds as subjects ■ Gerunds in parallel constructions ■ *Would* and *used to*	■ Omitting irrelevant information ■ Punctuating sentences with transitions and subordinating conjunctions	■ Distinguishing appropriate topics	■ Developing ideas	■ Technology for the Disabled
■ Comparatives and superlatives ■ *Both* and *neither* in comparisons ■ *While* to show contrast	■ Editing for correct use of comparatives and superlatives	■ Finding a basis of comparison	■ Listing ideas for a comparison	■ The Coffee Lover
■ Passive voice ■ Varying word order: *with* + noun phrase ■ Showing contrast: *Unlike* + noun phrase to show contrast ■ Giving reasons with *Because of* + noun phrase and *Because* + clause	■ Editing for correct use of passive voice	■ Speculating	■ Making comparisons interesting	■ Mapping the Human Genome
■ Using transitions and giving examples ■ Quotations and indirect speech ■ Generalizations	■ Editing for correct use of indefinite forms when making generalizations	■ Making a persuasive argument	■ Writing a five-paragraph essay exam	■ A New Treatment for Back Pain
■ Relative clauses (review)	■ Commas with nonrestrictive relative clauses ■ Reduced clauses	■ Distinguishing fact from opinion	■ Checking for mechanics	■ Bye, Bye, Charlie Brown
■ Conditional mood ■ Linking expressions and transition words	■ Editing for correct use of connectors	■ Determining realistic solutions	■ Making an outline for an essay	■ Justice and Racism

Chapter 1

Education and Student Life

IN THIS CHAPTER

You will write about the advantages of a large or small college.

PART 1

Before You Write

Exploring Ideas

Choosing a College

What Do You Think?

Ranking Arguments

When you write a paragraph giving your opinion on a topic, it is important to rank your arguments in order of importance. This helps persuade the reader to see your point of view.

Here are some reasons an immigrant or international student might choose a college in Canada or the United States. Which ones are most important to you? Rank them in order from 1 to 10, with 1 as the most important.

_____ class size

_____ facilities (libraries, laboratories)

_____ location

_____ quality of ESL classes

_____ number of international students

_____ special programs for international students

_____ courses offered

_____ cost

_____ ease of admission

_____ prestige

_____ help with job placement

1 Think about the list of reasons in the *What Do You Think?* box. What other reasons do you think are important to consider in choosing a college? List them below.

____

____

____

____

2 In small groups, discuss your ideas with other students. Tell why you thought certain reasons were important.

Building Vocabulary

3 In your discussion about choosing a college you may have heard some words you don't understand, or you may have found that you didn't know the English words for some of the ideas you wanted to express. Ask the teacher the meaning of any words you don't understand and add them to the following list.

Nouns	Verbs	Adjectives	Other
advantage	attend	impersonal	________
disadvantage	prefer	huge	________
facility		challenging	________
faculty		diverse	________
location			________
prestige			________
campus			________
tuition			________
scholarship			________

4 Match the vocabulary words in Activity 3 with the following words and phrases.

1. a good thing ________
2. the cost of college classes ________
3. very large ________
4. a good reputation ________
5. teachers ________
6. buildings, laboratories, libraries ________
7. go to ________
8. having many different kinds ________
9. not friendly ________
10. a bad thing ________

5 In small groups, discuss the advantages of large and small colleges. Consider some of the things in *What Do You Think?* on page 2. Write your ideas on the following lines.

Advantages of a Large College

____

____

____

Advantages of a Small College

____

____

____

6 Look at your lists of advantages. In small groups, discuss whether large or small colleges are better for non-native English speaking students.

7 Choose the topic you want to write about: the advantages of a large college or the advantages of a small college for immigrant or international students. Add to your list advantages other students mentioned that you think are important.

Organizing Ideas

Arranging Ideas in Order of Importance

Now that you have some ideas about your topic, you need to organize them. One way of doing this is to write about the most important ideas first, then the less important ones.

8 Look at the lists of advantages you made in Activity 5. Which advantages are most important? Rank these advantages in order of importance, with number 1 as the most important. Cross out any advantages that are not very important.

Giving Reasons

When you write, you should give reasons for your opinions. This helps to persuade the reader.

9 On the following lines, list your advantages in order of importance. Then give at least one reason for each of the advantages. This will make an outline you can use when you write.

Advantage 1: *Small schools have fewer students.*
Reason: *It is easier to get to know the other students.*

Advantage 1: ______________________________
Reason: ______________________________
Advantage 2: ______________________________
Reason: ______________________________
Advantage 3: ______________________________
Reason: ______________________________
Advantage 4: ______________________________
Reason: ______________________________
Advantage 5: ______________________________
Reason: ______________________________
Advantage 6: ______________________________
Reason: ______________________________

Writing Topic Sentences

The topic sentence usually comes at the beginning of a paragraph. It tells the reader the main idea of the paragraph. A good topic sentence is neither too specific nor too general.

10 Here is a list of possible topic sentences for a different paragraph about the advantages of studying abroad. Discuss them in groups or as a class. Are any topic sentences too specific or too general? There are several possible answers.

1. Students who study abroad often can't speak the language well.
2. Studying abroad has three main advantages.
3. There are several reasons why students should study abroad.
4. There are many good schools in foreign countries.
5. If possible, all college students should spend some time studying in a foreign country.

11 Write a topic sentence for your paragraph about the advantages of large or small colleges. It can be similar to one of the topic sentences on page 5.

12 Have another student read your topic sentence and discuss how you might improve it. Read the other student's topic sentence. Answer the following questions.

1. Is it a complete sentence?
2. Does it tell the reader what you are going to write about?
3. Is it too general or too specific?

PART 2 Write

Developing Cohesion and Style

A student and his advisor

Giving Reasons: Because, So, Therefore

When you give reasons for your ideas, you may want to use connectors that show cause or result.

- *Because* appears in phrases and clauses that state a cause (a reason).

  Examples

  Because large schools offer many different courses, students have a wide choice of subjects to take.

  Students have a wide choice of subjects to take *because* large schools offer many different courses.

- *So* and *therefore* appear in phrases and clauses that state a result.

  Examples

  Large schools offer many different courses. *Therefore,* students have a wide choice of subjects to take.

  Large schools offer many different courses, *so* students have a wide choice of subjects to take.

1 Complete the following sentences with *because, so,* or *therefore.* Note the different punctuation and capitalization in sentences with these three connectors.

1. Students who study in a foreign country live with people who do not speak their native language; _______________ they will learn a foreign language well.

2. Public colleges in your own state are more practical _______________ they are less expensive.

3. When students attend a local college, they can live at home _______________ they don't have to spend a lot on rent and food.

4. _______________ students have to study in a foreign language, they often have difficulty with their courses.

5. International students spend a long time away from home. _______________, they may forget their own customs and culture.

Using Transition Words: In addition, Also

When you write a paragraph that lists information, you must use transition words—words that connect your ideas. If you don't use transition words, your paragraph will sound "choppy"—that is, not smooth.

A writer can make a paragraph more cohesive by adding the transitions *also* and *in addition.*

Examples

It is very difficult to study abroad. *In addition,* it can be much more expensive than studying in your own country.

It is very difficult to study abroad. *Also,* it can be much more expensive than studying in your own country.

In addition usually comes at the beginning of a sentence. In this position, it always takes a comma.

Also can come at the beginning of a sentence, before a simple present or a past tense verb, or after an auxiliary verb or modal. If it comes at the beginning of a sentence, a comma always follows it.

2 Rewrite the following paragraph, using *also* and *in addition.*

Why Study Abroad?

Studying abroad offers students many advantages. The students live in a new culture, so they can learn both in and out of the classroom. They learn to be flexible because they have to adapt to different ways of living. They are far from home. Therefore, they have to become responsible and self-reliant. They have an experience they will remember all their lives.

3 Use transition words *in addition* and *also* to connect these pairs of ideas.

1. Undergraduate students are usually too immature to live away from home. They are too irresponsible.

____

____

____

2. Most students in four-year colleges are very intelligent. They study hard.

____

____

3. Professors in small colleges don't always understand international students. They may know very little about foreign cultures.

____

____

____

4. Students who go abroad to study lose close contact with their families. Some of them marry foreigners and never return home.

____

____

____

5. Studying in a foreign country is more exciting. You may get a better education.

____

____

Using Transition Words: First of all, Finally

Two other useful transitions are *first of all* and *finally.*

Examples

There are many reasons why international students feel homesick.

First of all, it may be the first time they are away from their families . . .

Finally, there is the problem of adapting to a completely different culture.

Note that *first of all* and *finally* always come at the beginning of a sentence and always take a comma.

Focus on Testing

The Importance of Transition Words

Activities 1, 2, and 3 in this section gave you practice with transition words. Transition words make your writing smooth and easy to read, so when you write a paragraph for a timed test, make sure you've used transition words correctly. Save time *after* you write to reread your paragraph. Make sure that each sentence connects logically to the one before it with an appropriate transition word.

4 Rewrite the following paragraph, using the transitions *in addition, also, first of all,* and *finally.* Remember to use commas where necessary.

There are several reasons that undergraduate students should not study away from home. Living away from home is much more expensive than living at home. Most teenagers are not mature enough to live far away from their families. Therefore, they often get into trouble. Many students feel lonely and homesick, so they are unable to study. Many who go away to study never return to their countries.

____

____

____

____

____

____

____

Avoiding Overgeneralizations

When you write, it is important not to make overgeneralizations, that is, statements that are so general that they are not true.

Examples of overgeneralizations:

International students work harder than North American students. (This is not always true!)

Teenagers are always irresponsible. (This is not always true!)

To avoid overgeneralizations:

- Don't use the adverbs of frequency *never* or *always*.
  - * Instead of *never*, use *rarely, hardly ever, almost never,* or *usually . . . not.*

    Example

    I *almost never* get sick.
  - * Instead of *always,* use *usually*, *almost always*, or *often*.

    Example

    Teenagers are *often* irresponsible.
- Don't use the quantifiers *no*, *none*, or *all*.
  - * Instead of *no* or *none,* use *very few, hardly any, almost no,* or *almost none.*

    Example

    Very few international students learn English easily.
  - * Instead of *all,* use *almost all, most, many,* or *some.*

    Example

    Many international students work harder than North American students.

5 Rewrite the following sentences to avoid generalizations, using adverbs of frequency and/or quantifiers.

1. International students have a difficult time their first year.

    ____

    ____

2. International students never become friendly with North Americans.

    ____

    ____

3. International students get better grades than North American students.

____

____

4. North American professors don't understand international students.

____

____

5. International students feel isolated.

____

____

6. Students in city colleges are too busy to be friendly.

____

____

7. Four-year colleges don't offer practical training.

____

____

8. Studying in a foreign language is always very difficult.

____

____

9. All students in community colleges can live at home.

____

____

10. Studying in a private college is extremely expensive.

____

____

Writing the First Draft

6 You have developed and organized your ideas and thought about the way you will write them. Now you are ready to write your paragraph. However, the paragraph you write will still need work; we call this paragraph a *draft.* A draft is an intermediate step, not the final product.

Write the first draft of your paragraph on the advantages of large or small colleges. Remember to include reasons for all of your opinions and to use transition words to connect your ideas. Write on every other line, so that it will be easy to make changes in your paragraph.

PART 3 Edit and Revise

Editing Practice

Editing for Content

You should edit your work at least two times.

- The first time, look for problems in the content and organization of the paragraph.
- The second time, focus on the form of the paragraph: on the writer's grammar, punctuation, and spelling.

1 Edit the following paragraph for content. Focus only on the writer's ideas and organization. Use the following questions to help you edit. Make any content corrections you think are necessary.

- Does the writer give enough information?
- Does the writer give a reason for each opinion?
- Does the topic sentence give the main idea of the paragraph?
- Are the writer's arguments organized from most important to least important?
- Does the writer use transition words and connectors?
- Does the writer use adverbs of frequency and quantifiers?

There are several reasons that undergraduate students should not study away from home living away from home is much more expensive than living at home. Teenagers are not mature enough to live far away from their families. Therefore, they often get into trouble. Many students feel lonely and homesick

So they are not able to study.

Editing for Form

Using Correct Paragraph Format

Here are some rules about the correct form of a paragraph. (For more rules on capitalization and punctuation, see Appendix 2 and Appendix 3.)

1. Indent the first sentence of your paragraphs.
2. Leave a left and right margin.
3. Begin each sentence with a capital letter.
4. End each sentence with a period (.), a question mark (?), or an exclamation mark (!).
5. Make sure that the end punctuation immediately follows the last word of the sentence.
6. Leave a small space between sentences.
7. Divide words between syllables. (A dictionary will tell you where to divide a word if you aren't sure where the syllables begin and end.)
8. Never divide one-syllable words.

2 Now edit the paragraph in Activity 1 a second time. This time, focus on the form. Use the rules in the preceding box to help you. Make any corrections you think are necessary. Then check your revised paragraph against the paragraph in Activity 4 on page 9.

Making General Statements with Present Tense Verbs

In English, there are several ways to make statements that are generally true. Look at the sentences in the activities in this chapter and answer these questions:

1. What tense are the verbs?
2. Are the subjects usually singular or plural?
3. Does the article *the* usually precede the subjects?

You will notice that general statements are in the simple present tense and that the subjects are usually plural with no articles. When the subjects are people, singular personal pronouns can be awkward in English. For example, look at these sentences. Which sentence sounds awkward? Why?

Students must leave their families.

A student must leave his or her family.

When you are editing compositions that contain general statements, make sure that you follow these rules:

1. Use simple present verbs.
2. Add *-s* to verbs with third-person singular subjects (*he, she,* or *it*).
3. Count nouns should generally be plural with no article. (You will learn more about the use of noncount nouns in Chapter 2.)
4. Pronouns must agree in number with their antecedents.
   Every student should keep his or her culture is correct although it is awkward.
   Every student should keep their culture would be wrong because *student* is singular.

3 The underlined words in the following sentences may be wrong. Edit the sentences according to the preceding four rules, changing the words that are incorrect. Some sentences may be correct.

1. Most <u>family save</u> for many years to send <u>his</u> children to college.

2. Students <u>feel</u> homesick.

3. Small schools don't have good library.

4. A large school has many students in their classes.

5. A school with many students aren't very friendly.

6. People who work can easily attend community colleges.

Editing Your Writing

4 Edit your first draft using the checklist below. First, check your paragraph for content, organization, cohesion, and style using items 1, 2, and 3 in the checklist. Then edit your paragraph for grammar and form using items 4 and 5.

Editing Checklist

1. Content
   a. Did you include everything that you wanted to say?
   b. Did you give a reason for each opinion?
2. Organization
   a. Does your topic sentence give the main idea of your paragraph?
   b. Did you organize your ideas from most important to least important?
3. Cohesion and Style
   a. Did you use transition words and connectors?
   b. Did you use adverbs of frequency and quantifers?
4. Grammar
   a. Did you use present tense verbs?
   b. Did you use adverbs of frequency and quantifers?
5. Form
   a. Did you use correct paragraph format? (indentation, division of words between syllables, margins)
   b. Did you use correct punctuation? (capitalization, commas, periods)
   c. Did you check the spelling of words you were not sure of?

Peer Editing

5 Show your paragraph to another student. She or he will check your work and tell you if anything is unclear.

Writing the Second Draft

6 After you edit your paragraph, rewrite it neatly, using correct form. Give your second draft to your teacher for comments. When your teacher returns your paper, ask him or her about any comments or corrections you don't understand. The next time you write, look back at your teacher's comments. Follow your teacher's instructions and try not to make the same mistakes again.

PART 4 A Step Beyond

Expansion Activities

1 Use the paragraphs the class wrote for this chapter for a debate.

1. Divide into two groups: students who think that small colleges are better for international students and students who prefer large colleges.
2. Meet with members of your team and read one another's compositions.
3. Make a list of your arguments.
4. Try to guess what the other team will argue and think of reasons against their arguments. (These are called *rebuttals.*)
5. Choose three students to represent each side. One gives the arguments (about five minutes), one the rebuttal (about three minutes), and one the summary (about three minutes).

2 Write another paragraph about the advantages or disadvantages of one of the following topics (or choose your own topic).

1. small towns / large cities
2. small families / large families

3 Look through some magazines and read the advertisements for different products. Choose an ad that shows a product's advantages. Make a list of all the advantages it describes. Give your list and the picture without the text to a partner. See if he or she can write the text using your list. Then compare your partner's ad with the real ad. How are they different? How are they the same?

Journal Writing

Start to keep a journal. In this journal, write whatever ideas come into your head. Your teacher may ask you to write in your journal in class or at home. Don't worry about grammar or correct form. Concentrate on expressing your ideas.

4 Choose one of the following topics to write about in your journal.

1. Start now and write for ten minutes about anything you want. If you can't think of anything to say, write about how you can't think of anything.
2. Write about your school and/or your English class. What do you like about it? What do you dislike? What do you find difficult? What is easy for you?

Video Activities: An Online English Class

Before You Watch. Discuss the following questions with your class or in a small group.

1. Do you ever use the Internet? What kinds of sites do you visit?
2. Do you ever do research for a paper online?
3. Have you ever taken an online course?
4. Do you know the expression "virtual reality"?

Watch. Check the following things students can do in Dr. Wesley's virtual English class.

1. _____ get announcements
2. _____ listen to a lecture
3. _____ link to Websites for research
4. _____ construct a personal web page
5. _____ take tests
6. _____ talk to classmates
7. _____ send an e-mail to the teacher

Watch Again. Virtual courses have both advantages and disadvantages. Compete the chart below. Afterwards, share answers with your classmates.

	Advantage(s)	Disadvantage(s)
For students		
For parents		
For teachers		

After You Watch. Use the chart above to summarize the advantages and disadvantages of online learning for one or more of the groups on the chart (students, parents, teachers). Use the transition words you learned in this chapter to connect the advantages and disadvantages. Give your opinion about online learning in your conclusion.

Chapter 2

City Life

IN THIS CHAPTER

You will write a description of the place where you live.

PART 1

Before You Write

Exploring Ideas

Describing Scenes

1 Look at these pictures of city streets and choose one of them to describe. Write as much as you can in ten minutes. You can answer some of these questions.

1. What is happening on the street?
2. How do you feel about the street?
3. How is the street similar to or different from the street where you live?

2 Form a small group with other students who wrote about the same picture. Discuss what you wrote. Did you notice the same things in the picture? Did you feel the same way about the street?

Including Sense Details and Feelings

You are going to write a personal description of the place where you live: your neighborhood, your street, your dormitory, your apartment or house, or your room. A good description includes *sense details:* the things you can see, hear, touch, taste, and smell.

What Do You Think?

Classifying Sense Details

Sense details make a description come alive. Work with a partner and test your knowledge of words used to describe things you see, hear, smell, taste, and touch. Classify the following adjectives by putting them in the correct category. (Note: Some might fit into more than one category.) Add some of your own.

noisy	salty	sour	dry	sticky	rotten
bitter	colorful	bright	sweet	dark	tight
rough	gloomy	foul	delicate		

see	**hear**	**smell**	**taste**	**touch**
________	________	________	________	________
________	________	________	________	________
________	________	________	________	________
________	________	________	________	________
________	________	________	________	________

Now think one thing that each word describes to show you know what it means.

3 Write the name of the place you are going to describe here (for instance, "My Neighborhood"):

____

4 Now make a list of sense details for the place you are going to describe.

1. What I can see:

   ____

   ____

2. What I can hear:

   ____

   ____

3. What I can touch:

   ____

   ____

4. What I can taste (optional):

   ____

   ____

5. What I can smell (optional):

   ____

   ____

5 A personal description also includes the feelings and opinions the writer has about the place he or she is describing. Write a few notes about *how* you feel about the place you describe. Also write about *why* you feel the way you do.

____

____

____

____

6 Describe the place you chose to a partner. Ask each other questions about the places you described.

Building Vocabulary

> If you use specific descriptive words, you can make your paragraph more interesting.

7 Read the following paragraph. Underline the descriptive words and phrases.

My Neighborhood

Since people from all over the world live in my neighborhood, it is a fascinating place to explore. When I walk down the main street of the neighborhood, I can hear the unfamiliar sounds of languages from all over the world. Each language is accompanied by a colorful ethnic shop or fascinating restaurant. On a warm evening, I can smell the sweet melons from the Korean vegetable store and the freshly baked bread from the Hungarian bakery. These smells are free, but for a small price I can also buy any of fifty kinds of cheeses with unpronounceable names from one store, or exotic Asian vegetables and the spices to liven them up from another. The people of the neighborhood take pride in their surroundings. They build neighborhood churches, synagogues, and clubs in all different architectural styles. On almost every street, they plant trees and flowers from their native countries to remind them of home and to brighten up the dreary gray cement and run-down apartment buildings. One neighbor of mine plants delicate Scottish flowers every year in memory of her mother's garden in Scotland. Another neighbor has a Chinese vegetable garden in window boxes. I don't need to buy an airplane ticket to experience the world; a walk around my neighborhood can be just as exciting.

---

8 Find words in the preceding paragraph that mean the following:

1. strange and unusual ____________________
2. small and pretty ____________________
3. bright ____________________
4. very interesting ____________________
5. to make pretty ____________________
6. sad-looking ____________________

9 Choose one of these pictures. In small groups, make lists of words that describe the neighborhood. Then use those words to describe the picture.

1. What you can see:

   ____

2. What you can hear:

   ____

3. What you can smell:

   ____

4. What you can taste:

   ____

5. What you can feel:

   ____

Organizing Ideas

Writing Topic Sentences

The topic sentence gives the main idea of a paragraph. It is often the first sentence in the paragraph. A topic sentence should

a. express an idea you can easily write about in one paragraph. The topic sentence should not be too general. If it is, there will be too much to write about, and you will need more than one paragraph.

b. have a clear *focus*. This means it should present a *particular* idea, feeling, or opinion about the topic.

Too general: My neighborhood is a nice place to live.

A good topic sentence: My neighborhood is fascinating because people from many countries live in it.

10 In each pair of topic sentences below, put an X next to the sentence that is too general and a check mark (✔) next to the one that has a clear focus.

1. Topic: "My Room"
   - a. _____ My room is a perfect place for one person to live.
   - b. _____ Many people live in single rooms.
2. Topic: "My House"
   - a. _____ There are a lot of houses like mine in my neighborhood.
   - b. _____ I love my house because it is filled with happy memories.
3. Topic: "My Dormitory"
   - a. _____ My dormitory has never felt like home to me.
   - b. _____ I live in a dormitory.

11 Write a topic sentence for your own paragraph. Then in small groups, discuss each others' topic sentences. Are any of them too general? Do they express a particular feeling or an opinion about the topic?

Adding Details to a Paragraph

The other sentences in a paragraph should develop the idea in the topic sentence. Look at the details that the writer will use to develop this topic sentence.

Topic sentence: My neighborhood is fascinating because people from many countries live in it.

- great shops—German butcher shop, Hungarian bakery, Korean produce store, French cheese store
- the food from the shops smells good
- ethnic restaurants
- many different languages
- woman next door plants flowers to remind her of Scotland
- beautiful churches and synagogues

A Ukrainian shop in New York City

12 Make notes you could use for sentences to develop your topic sentence. These notes are just ideas for you to think about. You don't have to use all the notes you make, and when you are writing your paragraph you may think of other ideas to write about.

____

____

____

____

Checking That All the Details Develop the Topic Sentence

All the details in the paragraph should develop the idea stated in the topic sentence.

13 In the following list, one detail is not related to the topic. Find it and cross it out.

Topic sentence: My room is small, but it is very cozy and has everything I need.

- is small but has enough space for my things, with a big closet
- has a big window with a view of a beautiful oak tree where there are often birds and squirrels
- landlord is not very pleasant
- is on the second floor and is quiet
- is nice and warm in winter
- has a small refrigerator and a cabinet for dishes

14 Look at the details you wrote for your paragraph and show them to a partner. Add any others you can think of and cross out the ones that are not on the topic.

Focus on Testing

Brainstorming for Ideas

In this section, you practiced writing topic sentences and adding details to a paragraph. When you're taking a test, you have little time to do these things. So take some time *before* you write to brainstorm. First, list all the ideas that come to your mind about the topic. Then read your list and see what main idea it suggests. (Cross out any ideas that don't fit.) Use your main idea to write a topic sentence. Use the rest of your ideas to develop your paragraph: group the ones that go together, and number them in the order you want to write about them.

Timed Activity: 8 Minutes

Choose a topic from the following. Then spend four minutes brainstorming ideas for the topic. First, write all your ideas down. Then go back and decide on a main idea. Next write a topic sentence. When you are finished, compare your topic sentence with a classmate's.

Topics

A description of your school

A description of your favorite place

Writing Concluding Sentences

Most paragraphs have concluding sentences, which may repeat the idea of the topic sentence in different words or give a personal reaction to the topic of the paragraph. Here is a concluding sentence for the ideas about the ethnic neighborhood in the box on page 23.

> I don't need to buy an airplane ticket to experience the world; a walk around my neighborhood is just as exciting.

Here is a good concluding sentence for a paragraph about how a Brazilian student felt about living in a dormitory with no other students from Brazil.

> I often felt lonely and homesick at first. However, I now know that I made some good American friends because I didn't have people from Brazil to talk with.

15 Give examples of some possible concluding sentences for these topics.

1. living in an apartment with two sloppy roommates

   ____

   ____

2. living in a run-down neighborhood where there's a lot of crime

   ____

   ____

3. living with your family

   ____

   ____

4. living in an old house

   ____

   ____

5. living in a small room in a modern dormitory

   ____

   ____

PART 2

Write

Developing Cohesion and Style

Giving Reasons: Since

Because and *since* have almost the same meaning. *Because* and *since* often appear in dependent clauses in complex sentences. Look at the following examples of complex sentences with *since.* The dependent clauses are underlined.

Examples

> *Since* quite a few people in the neighborhood come from Germany, there are many great German shops and restaurants here.
>
> There are many great German shops and restaurants here *since* quite a few people in the neighborhood come from Germany.

Note that a dependent clause with *since* can come at the beginning or the end of the sentence. If a clause with *since* begins a sentence, you usually use a comma after it. You don't use a comma if the clause comes at the end of the sentence.

1 Combine these sentences using *since.* Remember to use a comma after the clause if you put it at the beginning of the sentence.

1. Many people have lived in my neighborhood for years. It is a very friendly place.

   ____

   ____

2. My apartment is small. I have to keep it very neat.

   ____

   ____

3. My street is often dirty and smells like garbage. Many food stores are on it.

   ____

   ____

4. It is easy to get to know everyone in my dormitory. Only forty people live in it.

   ____

   ____

5. I have many relatives in the city. I decided not to live in a dormitory.

   ____

   ____

Varying Word Order in Sentences

If most of the sentences in a paragraph begin the same way, the paragraph may be boring to read. For example:

> My neighborhood is a wonderful place to eat and shop for food because people from all over the world live there. My neighborhood has a lot of different ethnic restaurants since the people come from many countries. My neighborhood is the best place to go when you want some good Chinese, Italian, Ukrainian, Vietnamese, or Polish food. My neighborhood is also the greatest when you want to buy many kinds of international foods. You can buy delicious cheeses and sausages at the Italian store on the corner of my block. You can buy sweet melons and all kinds fresh vegetables from the Korean produce store two blocks from my apartment. You can also buy freshly baked bread and pastries in the Hungarian bakery across the street. Why would I want to live anywhere else when everything I need is right in my neighborhood?

You can make the paragraph more interesting by varying the word order. For example, you can begin some of the sentences with dependent clauses (beginning with words like *because, since,* and *when*) or prepositional phrases (beginning with words such as *at, in, on, from, with*).

2 Rewrite the following sentences. Move the dependent clauses and prepositional phrases to the front.

1. I always see interesting people when I take a walk in my neighborhood.
   When I take a walk in my neighborhood, I always see interesting people.
2. I never liked Chinese food before I moved to this neighborhood.
   ______
3. I have become used to the sounds of traffic since I moved to the city.
   ______
4. You can find newspapers from all over the world on any street corner.
   ______
5. My neighbors are very friendly because everyone is from someplace else.
   ______

3 Look at the paragraph in Activity 7 on page 23. Underline the sentences that begin with dependent clauses or prepositional phrases. Look for words such as *because, since, when, at, in, on, from,* and *with.*

4 Rewrite the example paragraph from the box above. Vary the word order in some of the sentences to make the paragraph more interesting. Then, compare your paragraph with that of a classmate. Are your revised paragraphs similar?

Writing the First Draft

5 Write your paragraph using the topic sentence you wrote and the notes you made. Make your paragraph interesting by adding details and varying word order in your sentences. Don't worry about grammar when you write the first draft. Write on every other line so you can revise your paragraph.

PART 3

Edit and Revise

Editing Practice

Correcting Run-On Sentences

A run-on sentence is an incorrect sentence made of two independent sentences connected with a comma.

> *Run-on:* I am living in a dormitory room, it is much too small for my roommate and me.
>
> *Run-on:* First you notice all the exciting sights, later you notice the dirt.

You can correct a run-on sentence in at least three ways.

1. Change the comma to a period or a semicolon.

   I am living in a dormitory room. It is much too small for my roommate and me.

   First you notice all the exciting sights; later you notice the dirt.

2. Change the run-on sentence into a sentence with a dependent clause. The dependent clause is underlined in the example.

   I am living in a dormitory room <u>that is much too small for my roommate and me</u>.

   In the example above, the dependent clause describes the noun *dormitory room.* The pronoun *that* replaces *it.*

3. Use a conjunction such as *and, but,* or *so* to connect the two independent sentences. Note that a comma usually comes before the conjunction.

   First you notice all the exciting sights, *and* later you notice the dirt.

The following words often begin new sentences, but students sometimes use them after commas in run-on sentences. Check for them when you edit.

it he she they then however therefore later

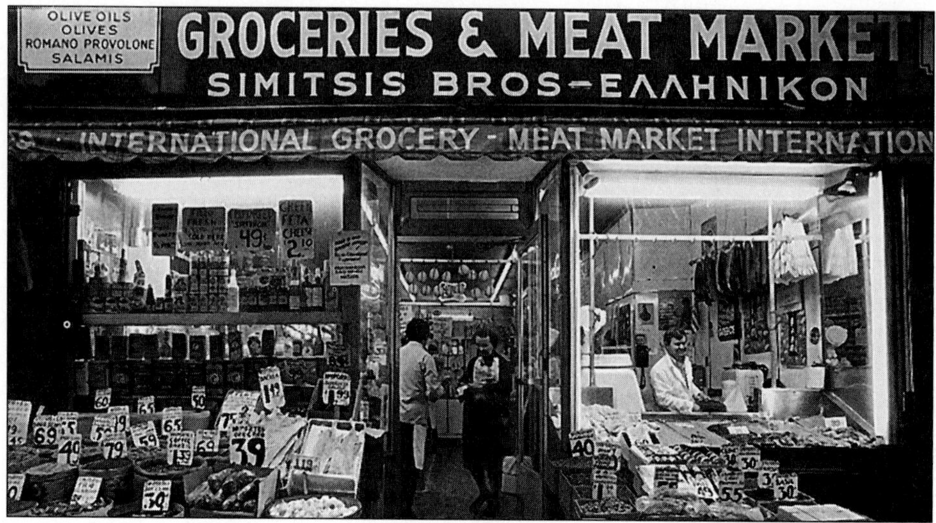

International products are available at this grocery store in New York City.

1 Correct these run-on sentences.

1. My suburban apartment is big and sunny, it has a living room with large windows filled with plants.
2. I have a roommate who is very sloppy, she never washes the dishes, and she leaves her clothes all over the apartment.
3. I like my street because my neighbors are wonderful, they will help anybody who is having problems.
4. First I painted my room a pale blue, later I made new curtains.
5. My favorite place to relax is the park, it is up the hill from my apartment.
6. My street is dirty and noisy, however it has many good restaurants and everyone on it is friendly.

2 Edit this paragraph for run-on sentences and rewrite it correctly.

My neighborhood is a fascinating place, it is in one of the biggest cities in the world, New York City, however, there is a small-town feeling to it. Most of the buildings in the neighborhood are small brick apartment houses, they have peeling red and brown paint. Many of the people here have lived in the neighborhood for years, they know each other and take pride in the neighborhood. They have planted trees and flowers in front of the buildings, they have built benches where the old people sit and talk. Since many of the people are from Germany and Eastern Europe, there are wonderful German, Hungarian, and Polish shops here. I wouldn't want to live in any other neighborhood of the city.

Editing with the Topic Sentence in Mind

All of the sentences in a paragraph should develop the main idea in the topic sentence. If they don't, there are two things you can do:

1. Maybe you started to write about an idea that is different from the idea in your topic sentence. If you like the idea, you should change your topic sentence.
2. Maybe some of your sentences are not about the idea in your topic sentence. You should cross out those sentences.

3 Revise the following paragraph. Should the writer change the topic sentence or cross out some sentences?

We live in an ordinary house on an ordinary street in an ordinary suburb, and I think it is terrific! Our house is now about thirty years old, but it looks newer. I used to live in apartments, first in Florida, and then in New Mexico. but I prefer living in our own home. My house is like hundreds of other houses in the suburbs, one story with an attached garage. There is nothing special about the house, and it won't win any prizes for architecture, but it's perfect for our family. The kitchen is big and has new appliances, including a washing machine and dryer. I hate the heat, but we have air conditioning in the living room and bedrooms, so it is always cool. I don't know why some people I know don't like the suburbs. For the kids there's a nice yard where they can play. It's very safe, so my wife and I don't have to worry. I am very thankful that we can afford this house and live our ordinary lives in it.

4 Edit this paragraph for form. Look for two run-on sentences, three misspelled words, and four tense errors.

My family live in a new neighborhood a few of miles from the center of a large city. Most of my neighbors came from the country. They leave their homes and families to get better jobs and more opportunities for their children. Because they used to live on farms, they like to live with nature. Plants cover every bit of their small front yards. Most of the houses are small, many of them are not finished yet. The houses are made of cement. Even though they are still building, they try to make their houses pretty, they paint them bright colors such as orange, purple and turquoise. Most of the families are working hard to earn money to finish their homes. The people in my neighborhood are very friendly and helpful to each other. In some ways, we are like immigrants in our own country.

Editing Your Writing

5 Edit your first draft using the following checklist. First, check your paragraph for content, organization, cohesion, and style, using items 1, 2, and 3 in the checklist. Then edit your paragraph for grammar and form, using items 4 and 5.

Editing Checklist

1. Content
   a. Did you add enough descriptive details?
   b. Did you use a variety of adjectives?
2. Organization
   a. Is your topic sentence the main idea of your paragraph?
   b. Do all the details develop the topic sentence?
   c. Did you include a concluding sentence?
3. Cohesion and Style
   a. Have you given reasons for your feelings?
   b. Have you varied the word order of your sentences?
4. Grammar
   a. Did you avoid run-on sentences?
   b. Did you use correct verb forms?
5. Form
   a. Did you use correct paragraph format? (indentation, division of words between syllables, margins)
   b. Did you use correct punctuation? (capitalization, commas, periods)
   c. Did you check the spelling of words you were not sure of?

Peer Editing

6 Exchange paragraphs with another student. Does she or he understand your paragraph? Does she or he think you need to make any corrections?

Writing the Second Draft

7 After you edit your paragraph, rewrite it neatly, using correct form. Give your second draft to your teacher for comments.

PART 4

A Step Beyond

Expansion Activities

1 Work in small groups. Take turns reading your paragraphs without their topic sentences. Your classmates will suggest some good topic sentences. Did anyone suggest a sentence that was similar to yours?

2 Look at the paragraphs in a description of your school (from a brochure or a school catalog) or in another reading selection. Try to find the topic sentence of each paragraph. Did some topic sentences come in the middle or the end of the paragraph? How many paragraphs had no topic sentences?

3 Find other descriptions of people, places, or things. Which descriptions are personal (including feelings and opinions)? Which descriptions are impersonal (including facts, not feelings)? Did the writer use sense details? If so, how?

4 Write a brief description of a common object—for example, a pencil, a brick wall, or a telephone. Don't write the name of the object, but include as many details as possible in the description. In small groups, take turns reading your descriptions. Can your classmates guess what you are describing?

Journal Writing

5 Write in your journal about one or both of the following topics.

1. Write two descriptions of a person you know. Write each description in ten minutes. Make the first impersonal, including only facts. Make the second personal, including feelings and opinions.

2. Chose a topic you would like your partner to write about in his or her journal. Write about the topic your partner chooses for you.

Video Activities: Garbage Car

Before You Watch. Discuss the following questions with your class or in a small group.

1. Where do you usually put the garbage from your home?
2. When trash is collected in your city, where does it go?
3. Why is it important to collect and dispose of trash properly?
4. Have you ever had a trash collection problem in the city where you live?

Watch. Watch the video and discuss the following questions with your classmates.

1. What was left in front of Ann Porter's home?
2. What is her problem?
3. Has the city where she lives tried to help her?
4. How does she feel?
5. Why is the situation dangerous?

Watch Again. Read the following statements. Write (T) if they are true and (F) if they are false.

1. _____ The car belongs to one of Ann Porter's neighbors.
2. _____ The car smells bad.
3. _____ The car has been in front of her house for a week.
4. _____ The police have come out to see the car.
5. _____ The car is a fire hazard.
6. _____ The city is going to take the car away tomorrow.

After You Watch. Pretend that you are Ann Porter. Write a letter of complaint to the city. First, describe the problem and say how you feel about it. Second, tell the city what you want them to do about the problem. You can begin like this:

> Dear Sir or Madam,
>
> Two weeks ago, someone left a filthy, smelly old station wagon in front of my house. . . .

Chapter 3

Business and Money

IN THIS CHAPTER

You are going to write a letter to the editor in response to a newspaper article.

PART 1

Before You Write

Exploring Ideas

Discussing Attitudes Toward Money

1 Read these famous quotations and proverbs about money. In small groups, discuss the sayings. Do you agree with them or not? What attitude toward money does each one express?

> If possible, make money honestly; if not, make it by any means.
> —*Horace (65–8 B.C.)*
>
> If you would know the value of money, go and try to borrow some; for he that goes a-borrowing goes sorrowing. Time is money.
> —*Benjamin Franklin (1706–1790)*
>
> Money speaks sense in a language all nations understand.
> —*Aphra Behn (1640–1689)*
>
> Money is our madness, our vast collective madness.
> —*D. H. Lawrence (1885–1930)*
>
> It has been said that the love of money is the root of all evil.
> —*Samuel Butler (1835–1902)*
>
> Money buys everything except love, personality, freedom, immortality, silence, peace.
> —*Carl Sandburg (1878–1967)*

2 Think of another quotation or proverb about money. Discuss the quotations with a partner. What attitudes toward money do they show?

3 Write as much as you can in ten minutes about your own attitude toward money.

4 In small groups, read the following newspaper article and discuss the different people's reactions to the event it describes. You are going to write a letter to the editor in response to it.

Luck or Thievery?

COLUMBUS, OHIO. October 28 was a lucky day for motorists driving along Interstate 71 at about 9:30 in the morning. As a truck from the Metropolitan Armored Car Company sped down the highway, its back door blew open, spilling bags of money onto the road. When other vehicles hit the bags, they split open, spewing out a million dollars.

It didn't take motorists long to realize that the paper swirling around them was hard cash. They stopped on and around the highway and scooped up handfuls of money, gleefully cramming \$20, \$50, \$100, even \$1,000 dollar bills into bags, pockets, and purses. When the police arrived, they estimated that two hundred people were helping themselves to this bonanza.

Officials hoping to recover this money were not so gleeful. Columbus Mayor Dana G. Rinehart called these people thieves and said, "May they have many sleepless nights." He claims the government will prosecute anyone the police can find.

To encourage the return of the money, Metropolitan Armored Car has offered a reward of 10% of all the money they receive. So far, however, they have received only \$100,000—from about thirty different people. One man turned in \$57,000. Another man, however, called to say he was set for life and was leaving town. Since the cash was insured and belonged to local banks, many people can't see that they are hurting real people by keeping it.

Even if the government prosecutes, it will have trouble convicting the thieves. "Probably two-thirds of the jurors would think the defendant should have kept the money," said prosecutor Michael Miller.

Building Vocabulary

5 Underline these words in the newspaper article above. Use the context to help you guess the meaning. Then match the words with their meanings.

1. _h_ armored	a. very happy
2. _____ split	b. pick up
3. _____ spew	c. charge with a crime
4. _____ swirl	d. tear open
5. _____ scoop up	e. move in circles
6. _____ gleeful	f. spill
7. _____ bonanza	g. sudden riches
8. _____ prosecute	h. protected with strong metal
9. _____ convict	i. find guilty of a crime

6 In your response to the article, you might want to use some of the words that you weren't familiar with. First categorize them into parts of speech. Then make sentences with six of the words, giving your opinion of the happenings in the article.

Nouns	Verbs	Adjectives
______	______	armored
______	______	______
______	______	______
______	______	______
______	______	______

Example

Maybe the drivers of the *armored* car didn't lock the doors intentionally.

Organizing Ideas

Writing Reactions to a Reading Selection

7 Discuss these questions in small groups.

1. Is it wrong to keep money that you haven't earned?
2. What does it mean that the money is *insured*? Who will pay back the money? Is it true that the loss of the money doesn't hurt anyone?
3. What would you do if you were one of the motorists? Would you take the money? What would you do if you were an official of the town?

8 Should the motorists return the money? Write reasons why or why not.

Reasons Why the Motorists Should Return the Money

____

____

____

____

____

____

Reasons Why the Motorists Should Not Return the Money

____

____

____

____

____

____

9 Read what you wrote about your attitude toward money in Activity 3 on page 38. Do you think the motorists should or should not return the money? Does your attitude toward money support your opinion?

Analyzing the Organization of a Letter to the Editor

10 Read this letter to the editor of a newspaper. Then answer the questions that follow.

Regarding the report on people who don't pay taxes on money they make from small home businesses (Oct. 23): My opinion is that the government should stay out of at least one part of our lives.

First of all, most people who run these small businesses are law-abiding citizens. Many of them have other jobs where they pay more than their share of taxes (unlike the wealthy, who pay almost none). Others are people who want jobs where they have to pay taxes, but can't find them.

Secondly, the government requires too much paperwork from small businesses. If these small businesspeople have to keep the complicated records that the tax people require, they won't have time to sell old furniture, prepare food for parties, or whatever their business involves.

Finally, and most importantly, this is supposed to be a free country, but the government interferes everywhere. Let us be free at least in our own homes!

Al Melinowski

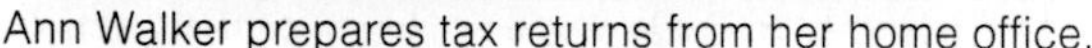

Ann Walker prepares tax returns from her home office.

Mike Brukowski caters parties from his home kitchen.

1. How does the letter begin and end?
2. How many paragraphs does the letter have? Are the paragraphs long or short? (Note that paragraphs in newspapers are often shorter than paragraphs in academic writing.)
3. What transition expressions does the writer use?
4. How does the writer support his opinions?

11 Write an opening sentence for your letter responding to "Luck or Thievery" similar to the opening sentence of "Home Free." Begin with a phrase telling which article you are responding to: *"Regarding . . ."* or *"In response to . . ."* Give the name and date of the article and then tell your opinion.

12 Now give two or three reasons for your opinion:

PART 2

Write

Developing Cohesion and Style

Stating Obligations and Opinions with Modals: Must, Have to, Should, Ought to

You can show the strength of your opinion by the modal you use.

Examples

You *should* do your homework every night.
We *have to* turn in our papers tomorrow.
I *ought to* get a job. I need some extra money.
They *must* arrive on time or we will leave without them.

1 Which of the modals *must, have to, should,* and *ought to* show strong obligation? Which show weaker obligation? Find an example of *should* and an example of *have to* in the letter to the editor on page 41. Why do you think the writer used those modals?

2 Make sentences using *must, must not, have to, not have to, should, should not,* or *ought to* about the following topics, depending on how strong you think the obligation is.

Example

Everyone should give money to charity but many people don't.

1. paying taxes
2. drinking alcohol and then driving
3. spending a lot of money to clean up the environment
4. giving money to the poor
5. gambling
6. trying to find the owner of some jewelry you found on the street
7. robbing a person's house if you need money
8. borrowing someone's car

Supporting an Opinion with a General Statement and Examples

A general truth is a statement of opinion that most people would agree with.

Most people would like to have more money. That is why lotteries are so popular.
general truth — supporting example

3 Look at the second paragraph in the letter to the editor on page 41. It gives a general truth and then supports it with examples. What is the general truth? What are the examples?

General truth: ______________________________

Examples: ______________________________

____

4 These sentences state general truths. Give one or two examples to support them.

1. The government loses millions of dollars every year because of people who don't pay their share of taxes.

   Many rich people pay no taxes at all.

   ____

2. Almost everyone gambles in one way or another.

   ____

   ____

3. The love of money is the root of all evil.

   ____

   ____

4. Lack of money is the root of much of the evil of our society.

   ____

   ____

5. When you find something on the street that someone has lost, it is almost impossible to find the owner.

   ____

   ____

5 Look at the reasons you gave in Activity 8 on page 41 for your opinion on the newspaper article. Can you support any of them with examples?

Supporting an Opinion with Predictions

6 Look at the third paragraph in the letter to the editor on page 41. It supports a general statement with a prediction. What is the prediction?

____

What verb tense is used in the *if* clause?

____

What verb tense is used in the main clause?

____

7 In small groups, make predictions. What will happen if . . .

1. the government opens (or closes) gambling casinos in your city?
2. the government starts (or prohibits) a lottery in your city?
3. the government makes the wealthy pay more taxes?
4. the government cuts welfare payments?
5. everyone gives one-tenth of his or her income to charity?
6. there are fewer drunk drivers on the road?
7. the government makes smoking completely illegal in your town?
8. someone tries to return a valuable item he or she found on the street?

8 Look at the reasons you gave for your opinion on the newspaper article. Can you support any of them with predictions?

Focus on Testing

Supporting Your Opinion

In this section, you've seen two ways to support an opinion. If you know you are going to take a timed test that requires you to give your opinion, it's a good idea to come to the test prepared to support it. To do this, think of topics you have covered in class or read news magazines to find current topics of interest *before* the test. Practice stating your opinion and supporting it with predictions or examples. This way, you'll be more comfortable with thinking of supporting reasons under time pressure.

Timed Activity: 5 Minutes

Choose a topic from the following list. Give yourself five minutes to decide on your opinion and brainstorm predictions and examples to support it.

Everyone Needs a College Education
Education Should Be Free for Everyone
Lotteries Should Be Illegal
Democracy Is Not Always the Best Form of Government

9 Compare your predictions and examples with those of another student who chose the same topic. Which items are similar? Which are different?

Stating Opinions: Strong and Moderate

Some letters to the editor express opinions strongly and others do so moderately. A strong opinion does not usually allow for different points of view, whereas a moderate opinion does. When writers express their opinions strongly, they often use more emotional arguments. When writers express their opinions moderately, they often use more logical arguments.

10 Read the following expressions. Which of them are strong? Which are more moderate? How can you tell?

	Strong	Moderate
1. I disagree with . . .	______	✔
2. . . . is total nonsense.	______	______
3. My opinion is that . . .	______	______
4. . . . is immoral.	______	______
5. . . . is the most logical solution.	______	______
6. Only a fool would disagree with . . .	______	______
7. I believe . . .	______	______
8. In my opinion . . .	______	______
9. . . . is completely absurd.	______	______

11 Create some sentences about the newspaper article using the expressions in Activity 10. Which do you think are more appropriate for your letter?

Writing the First Draft

12 Write your letter using the opening sentence in Activity 11 on page 42. Give your opinions and the reasons for your opinions, supporting them with examples or predictions. Don't worry about grammar. Write on every other line so you can revise your paragraph. Add transitions to your paragraph.

PART 3 Edit and Revise

Editing Practice

Avoiding Faulty Reasoning

When you revise a piece of writing that gives reasons for opinions, you should make sure that you haven't used *faulty reasoning.* Following are definitions and examples of different kinds of faulty reasoning.

1. False analogy: comparing two things that are not similar

   Example

   Some people have to gamble.

   They are just like thieves because they can hurt other people.

2. Generalization: saying that something is true for all when it is only true for some, or making a general statement based on only a few cases

   Example

   There is a wealthy man who comes into the restaurant where I am a waiter and never leaves a tip. Rich men aren't generous.

   (Note that in this example the generalization follows the description of one particular case.)

3. Irrelevant argument: giving an example or reason that does not relate to the opinion

   Example

   I don't think the accountant was embezzling money from her company because she is so nice.

   She always says hello to me.

   An irrelevant argument might also suggest that because one thing follows another, it relates to it, when it really doesn't.

   Example

   Borrowing money always causes problems.

   Two days after Mario borrowed money, his wife asked for a divorce.

4. Begging the question: giving a reason that only restates the opinion in different words.

   Example

   Gambling is wrong because it is immoral.

1 The following statements are responses to the newspaper article you read, "Luck or Thievery." Identify the kind of faulty reasoning each one shows.

1. Everyone should return the money because the money should go back to the government.
2. I heard about a woman who got some of the money and didn't return it. The next day she fell and broke her leg. She knew she did the wrong thing.
3. Insurance companies always cheat people.
4. Picking up the money that fell onto the road is similar to picking flowers that grow in the forest.

2 Look at the reasons and examples you wrote in your letter. Do any of them show faulty reasoning?

What Do You Think?

Evaluating Arguments for Faulty Reasoning

Evaluating an argument for faulty reasoning is an important critical thinking skill. Practice this skill by listening to a talk show program on the radio or TV, or reading a letter to the editor in a newspaper. Take notes on the person's opinion and the reasons given for her or his opinion. Discuss your notes in small groups. Discuss whether or not the person used faulty reasoning.

Correcting Spelling Errors

Always edit your writing for spelling errors. This is a good time to review the spelling rules in Appendix 1. However, you can't always count on rules to help you with spelling. Often you have to use a dictionary to check words you are not sure you have spelled correctly.

3 Correct these words if they are incorrect or write *correct* if they are correct. Use your dictionary if you are not sure.

1.	successful	correct	6.	estimatted	________
2.	moralety	________	7.	defendant	________
3.	evil	________	8.	prosecutor	________
4.	honnestly	________	9.	government	________
5.	truely	________	10.	taxs	________

Correcting Syllabification Errors

General Rules for Syllabification

1. If a word is too long to fit at the end of the line, divide it between syllables and put the second part of the word on the next line.
2. Put at least three letters on each line, and use a hyphen after the first part of the divided word.
3. Don't divide words that have one syllable.
4. Divide words after prefixes or before suffixes.

   con-struc-tion em-bez-zle-ment com-fort-a-ble
5. Divide words between two consonants.

   col-lege ad-dic-tion com-pul-sive
6. If you are not sure how to divide a word, write the whole word on the next line or check your dictionary.

Look at these examples:

Incorrect: We couldn't find the place they told us about.

Correct: We couldn't find the
place they told us about.

Incorrect: He's always borrowing money.

Correct: He's always borrowing money.

or:

He's always bor-
rowing money.

4 If these words didn't fit at the end of a line, how would you divide them? Draw a line between syllables. Check your dictionary if necessary.

1. expensive
2. accounting
3. irrelevant
4. organization
5. consumer
6. generous
7. argument
8. immoral

5 Edit the following paragraph. Find seventeen spelling errors, four syllabification errors, and three run-on sentences.

A Problem with Priorities

Pacific College spends too much money on activitys that are
not related to educattion. One of the bigest expenses is ath-
letics, for example, it has to pay for coaches' saliries, e-
quipment, and building stadiems. It also sponsors a free student newspaper and many student activaties such as partys,
plays, and conserts. Many staf members spend a lot of time o-
rganizing and planing these activities, they have to be paid
salaries for this work as well. These activatys are fine, but
not when the college is decresing libery hours on the weekends and increasing class size I like football games, partys,
and conserts, but I beleive that my educattion is more important.

Editing Your Writing

6 Edit your letter using the following checklist. First, check your paragraph for content, organization, cohesion, and style, using items 1, 2, and 3 in the checklist. Then edit your paragraph for grammar and form, using items 4 and 5.

Editing Checklist

1. Content
   a. Did you state your opinion clearly?
   b. Did you support your opinion with reasons?
   c. Did you support your reasons with examples and/or predictions?
   d. Did you avoid faulty reasoning?
2. Organization
   a. Did you write an opening sentence that told what article you were responding to and that gave your opinion?
   b. Did you write a concluding sentence?
3. Cohesion and Style
   a. Did you use transitions?
   b. Did you state your opinions using appropriate modals?
   c. Did you use a moderate or a strong style to express your opinions?
4. Grammar
   a. Did you use simple verb forms with modals?
   b. Did you use present verb forms in *if* clauses and future verb forms in predictions?
   c. Did you avoid run-on sentences?
5. Form
   a. Did you use correct paragraph format: indentation, margins, capitals at beginning of sentences?
   b. Did you use correct spelling and syllabification?

Peer Editing

7 Exchange papers with a classmate and edit each other's paragraphs. Circle or underline in pencil any words, phrases, or sentences that you don't understand or that you think need to be corrected. Then return your paragraphs. Discuss any questions you have with your partner.

Writing the Second Draft

8 After you edit your letter, rewrite it neatly, using correct form. Sign your name and write your city at the bottom.

PART 4 A Step Beyond

Expansion Activities

1 Tape your letters to the board in two groups: one group for letters saying that the people should give the money back, and another group for the letters saying that the people shouldn't. Go to the board and read some of the letters. What reasons were given for each opinion? Are you and your classmates in general agreement or are there many differing opinions?

2 Read some letters with opinions opposite to yours. Make a list of reasons why their arguments are not logical or true. Then get into teams and have a debate on the topic. (Students not on the debate teams can be the audience.) Students on both teams take turns presenting the reasons for their opinions; then both teams give their counter arguments. Finally, each team sums up. The audience can vote on which side won the debate.

3 Look at a local, international, or school newspaper or magazine and the letters to the editor. Often some are logical and others are emotional; some are serious and others try to be funny. Which letters do you like? Do they give strong or moderate opinions?

4 Find an article or letter in a newspaper and write a letter in response to it.

5 Have you experienced or heard about a strange happening like the one described in the newspaper article in this chapter? Write a description of the happening. Share your description with a classmate.

Journal Writing

6 Write in your journal about one or more of these topics.

1. Write a letter to your teacher telling him or her what you like about the writing course and what you have learned. Then write about a suggestion you have for improving the course. You can give this to your teacher if you like.
2. Write your reaction to one of the proverbs or sayings at the beginning of this chapter or to one a classmate has told.
3. Write the word "BUSINESS" in the center of a page. Then quickly, without thinking, write around it any words, phrases, or ideas you associate with the word. Use some of these words or ideas to write about your opinion of business.

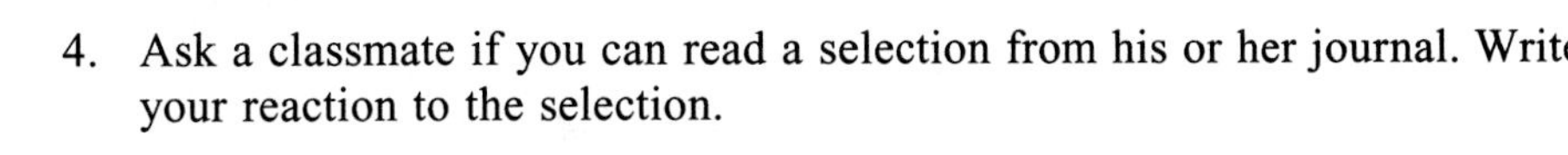

4. Ask a classmate if you can read a selection from his or her journal. Write your reaction to the selection.

Video Activities: A Teenage Stockbroker

Before You Watch. Discuss the meanings of the following words and expressions with your classmates. Check the meanings in a dictionary if necessary. Then complete the definitions below.

1. Stocks and shares Stocks and shares are kinds of ________________
2. Stock exchange A stock exchange is ________________
3. Investor An investor is a person who ________________
4. Risk For an investor, a risk means ________________

Watch. Discuss the following questions with your classmates

1. Talk about Dan. How old is he? What is unusual about him?
2. Where is Dan standing at the beginning of the video?

Watch Again. Read the following statements. Write (T) if they are true and (F) if they are false.

1. _____ Dan has been trading stocks for six years.
2. _____ Dan has never lost money on the stock market.
3. _____ Dan dropped out of high school and now spends all his time trading stocks.
4. _____ Dan publishes all his wins and losses on his Website.
5. _____ Dan plans to buy a house in Malibu (California) when he is 19.

After You Watch. Imagine that you are Dan, a 17-year-old millionaire. This year you are going to graduate from high school. What's next? In your journal, write about your plan for the next five years. Some questions to think about before you write:

- Are you going to go to college?
- Where are you going to live?
- What are you going to do with your money?
- How do you think your life is going to change?

Write in the first person, as if you were Dan.

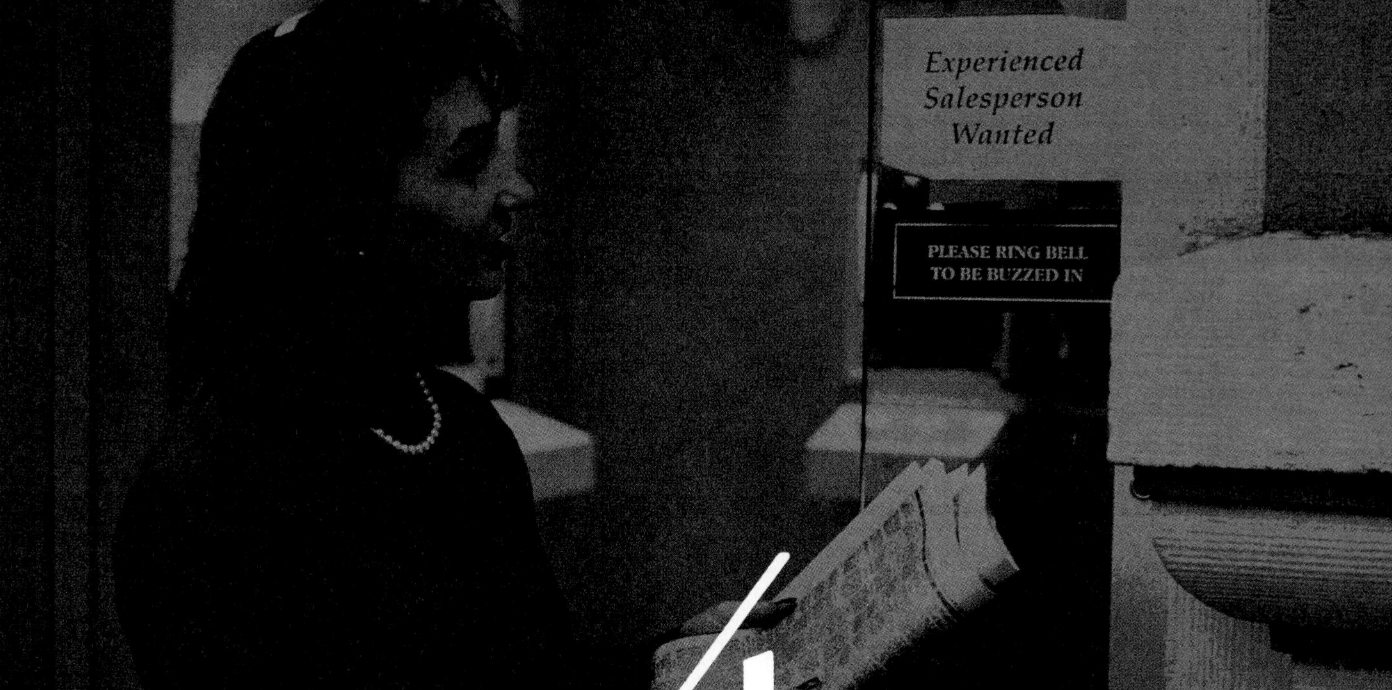

Chapter 4

Jobs and Professions

IN THIS CHAPTER

You are going to write a reply to this job or college application instruction: *Describe an accomplishment in your life.*

PART 1

Before You Write

Exploring Ideas

Discussing Accomplishments

On application forms (and during personal interviews), many colleges and employers ask applicants to describe some personal accomplishments. In discussing personal accomplishments, you want to show that you are special or different in some way. You should be positive and focus on your good points. Give enough information to show how you are special, but not too much: you don't want to seem as if you are exaggerating or bragging.

1 Look at these instructions from parts of college and job applications. As a class or in small groups, discuss the reactions of the students in the pictures to the question *"What have you accomplished in the past two years?"* What do you think about their reactions? Do you feel similarly about this question?

- What have you accomplished in the past two years?
- Tell us something about yourself that will help us know you better.
- Write a short personal history.
- Write about the most difficult thing you have ever done.
- Discuss your duties in your previous or present job.

2 As a class or in small groups, discuss the attitudes toward describing accomplishments in your country. Do employers and colleges expect you to focus on your successes or do they expect you to be humble and not tell much about your successes? What should you avoid discussing (for example, religion, which is a private matter in some countries)?

Building Vocabulary

3 The following words and phrases describe personal characteristics. In small groups, discuss their meanings. Put a check mark (✔) next to the positive words. Put an X next to the negative words. Put a question mark (?) next to words that you are not sure about.

_____ ambitious
_____ concerned about other people
_____ creative
_____ disciplined
_____ enthusiastic
_____ hardworking
_____ jealous
_____ aggressive
_____ a good sense of humor
_____ self-confident
_____ agreeable
_____ moody
_____ trustworthy
_____ cold
_____ sensitive

What Do You Think?

Implying Qualities

One way to write about an accomplishment is to *imply*—that is, suggest indirectly—that you have certain qualities such as intelligence, honesty, and humor. You can demonstrate that you have these qualities by describing your experiences and what you have learned from them. This way, the reader will infer that you have a particular quality. If you show how you solved a difficult problem, for example, the reader can make the inference that you are smart and creative.

Practice thinking up ways to imply particular qualities. Work with a partner. Together, think of situations that might lead a reader to infer the following qualities in a person:

intelligence courage humor patience honesty creativity

4 In small groups, choose three of the following people and discuss how their experiences show that they have characteristics that are important to success in work and school.

1. Miguel's mother works afternoons, so Miguel has taken care of his younger brother after school for the last four years.
2. Yoshi taught himself how to play the guitar and plays in a band.
3. Greta works as a salesclerk in her uncle's store.
4. Shenner has been studying English for the last nine months with money he got from a scholarship as the top student in his class.
5. Paulo likes to create computer games.
6. Ana is a bicyclist and takes long trips on her bicycle.
7. Sophia has been raising three children for the last eight years.
8. All of Parvin's friends tell her their problems.

5 Discuss one or two experiences you could write about on a job or college application form. How does the experience show you have qualities that are important for success?

6 Write notes about the experience you think best shows that you have accomplished or learned something. Answer these questions:

1. What did you do?
2. What was difficult about the experience?
3. How did you face the difficulty?
4. What did the experience teach you?
5. What qualities does the experience show you have?
6. What did you accomplish through the experience?

Organizing Ideas

Limiting Information

7 Look at the beginning of a first draft of a personal description. The writer hasn't limited what he wants to say. Is it easy to read? Cross out the information he should leave out.

I have learned a lot working as a bike messenger in New York City. First of all, I have learned to persevere when there are difficulties. I also find math very difficult, but I have a tutor now who has been a great help to me. Many times I have wanted to quit, but I have tried to keep my sense of humor. I have had problems with drivers who almost run me over, constant rain for weeks at a time, unreadable addresses, and rude customers. I think the drivers in New York are the worst in any city I have seen. I have also learned that even the most routine job can be interesting.

---

8 Look at the notes you made in Activity 6. Cross out any information that does not demonstrate what you have accomplished or learned.

9 You will probably be able to write about your experience in one paragraph. However, if the experience has several parts, you might want to use two paragraphs. For example, you might write in one paragraph about how you worked when your job was starting, and in the second paragraph about how you changed to face a problem you were experiencing. Look at your notes again. Do you think you will write everything in one paragraph or two? (You may change your mind after you begin writing.)

Writing Topic Sentences

> The topic sentence for your paragraph should make the reader interested in you. It should show how you're special and should be positive, focusing on your good points.

10 These are topic sentences some students wrote for their paragraphs. Discuss them in small groups. Which ones do you like? Why?

1. I have always danced just for fun, but I recently realized that dancing has been an important learning experience for me.
2. I guess a lot of people take care of their children, so it isn't very special.
3. Two years ago, my family and I immigrated to Vancouver, Canada, and my life changed.
4. A very important thing has been happening.
5. Although I was born in Vietnam, I have been living in a small town in Texas for the last three years, and the two cultures have affected me in many important ways.
6. My relationship with my children has developed my creativity, discipline, and sense of humor.
7. Last year I had a very bad experience.
8. I like to go swimming a lot.

Writing Concluding Sentences

> The kind of paragraph you will write needs a concluding sentence. It can tell what you learned about yourself from the experience you chose, or it can describe a hope for the future. It should leave the reader with a positive feeling.

11 Discuss these concluding sentences in small groups. Which ones are effective? Why? Which ones are not? Why not?

1. I guess raising children isn't easy for anyone.
2. I can never do things I don't enjoy, but when I like something I work pretty hard at it.
3. I hope that my experience raising my own children will help me be a better teacher.
4. I feel that I've experienced the best of both cultures, and I hope to use this experience in my future work.
5. I never want to go through such a horrible experience again.
6. Now I know that if I enjoy something and know it is important, I can work really hard to make it a success.

12 In small groups, tell the other students what experience you are going to write about. Discuss some possible concluding sentences you might use.

PART 2 Write

Developing Cohesion and Style

Using the Correct Tense: Past Versus Present Perfect

Guidelines for Choosing Past or Present Perfect

PAST TENSE

Shows *completion* of action, state, or time period, especially when the past time is mentioned.

Example

I *was* in Boston for Christmas vacation in 2000. (The time is completed and is mentioned.)

PRESENT PERFECT TENSE

Shows *incompletion* of action, state, or time period—especially when the exact time of the past action is not important.

Example

I **have gone** to Boston for Christmas vacation many times. (Exactly when is not important.)

Every year since 1999 I **have gone** to Boston for Christmas vacation. (I still go.)

1 Choose the correct tense of the verb, past or present perfect, for these sentences. To choose, ask yourself these questions: "Is the action or state completed? If a time is mentioned, is that time completed or not?"

Examples

(You live in Tokyo.) I ___have lived___ (live) in Tokyo for three years.

(You live in New York.) I ___lived___ (live) in Caracas for three years.

1. My father ________________ (come) to visit me once a year since 1997.
2. My mother ________________ (come) to visit me next year.
3. I ________________ (have) two jobs this year.
4. I ________________ (have) two jobs last year.
5. (You have immigrated.) I ________________ (learn) a lot when I was waiting to immigrate.
6. I ________________ (learn) a lot in my life.
7. I ________________ (work) in this store for a month now.
8. I ________________ (work) in a store for a month, but then I quit.
9. Kelsey ________________ (take) dance classes last year.
10. She ________________ (take) dance classes for one year.
11. Eduardo ________________ (be) to Mexico City many times.
12. He ________________ (be) to Mexico City two years ago.

Using the Correct Tense: Present Perfect Versus Present Perfect Continuous

Guidelines for Choosing Present Perfect or Present Perfect Continuous

Present Perfect

The present perfect tense describes actions or situations that happened at an *unspecified* time in the past.

Example I have been to San Francisco. (The time is not specified.)

The present perfect tense also describes *repeated past* actions. The following time expressions often appear with the present perfect tense: *already, just, recently, still, yet, twice, three (four,* etc.*) times.*

Examples I have visited San Francisco three times.

My parents have just returned from Europe.

Present Perfect Continuous

The present perfect continuous tense describes actions or situations that began in the past and have continued to the present or are still true in the present. This tense emphasizes *continuous* or *ongoing* activity; the following time expressions often appear with it: *so far, up to now, for* (a period of time), or *since* (a beginning time).

Examples I have been going to that restaurant for months.

We have been swimming a lot this summer.

Present Perfect Versus Present Perfect Continuous

With nonaction verbs—verbs that express feelings, opinions, possession, or perceptions—use the present perfect tense to describe actions or situations that began in the past and have continued to the present or are still true in the present. The following are examples of different kinds of nonaction verbs: *be, believe, know, like, need, prefer, seem, realize, want.*

Possession: *belong to, have, own, possess*

Perceptions: *wear, smell, look, taste, see*

Examples They have known about this meeting since last month.

I haven't seen her for years.

A few verbs, such as *live, make, study, think,* and *work,* are used with the present perfect continuous or the present perfect with little difference in meaning when a time expression is used.

Examples She has worked at this company for five years.

She has been working at this company for five years.

We have lived here since 1998.

We have been living here since 1998.

2 Choose the correct tense, present perfect or present perfect continuous. First ask yourself if the verb is nonaction. If it is an action verb, ask yourself if the sentence stresses continuous or ongoing action.

Examples

I ___have known___ about this for a long time.

I ___have been thinking___ about this since yesterday.

1. He ____________ (work) with me since 1988—we still work together at the same place.
2. Has he ever ____________ (work) in a restaurant?
3. I ____________ (not write) my essay yet.
4. I usually write every day, but I ____________ (not write) much lately.
5. She ____________ already ____________ (fill out) her application.
6. She ____________ (fill out) her application for the last four hours.

3 Complete these paragraphs with the simple past, present perfect, or present perfect continuous forms of the verbs in parentheses.

I ___have liked___ (1) (like) to write since I ____________ (2) (be) five years old. When I first ____________ (3) (hold) a pen in my hand and carefully ____________ (4) (draw) the beautiful Japanese characters, I ____________ (5) (know) I ____________ (6) (want) to be a writer. Ever since that day I ____________ (7) (write) in my free time. When I ____________ (8) (come) to Miami six months ago to study English, I ____________ (9) (not realize) I would feel so frustrated. I ____________ (10) (have) the thoughts of a nineteen-year-old but the skills of a three-year-old!

Although I ____________ (11) (study) hard since that day, I still ____________ (12) (not write) an essay in English I can be proud of. This experience _______________ (be) frustrating, but I _______________ (learn) a lot from it. For six months, I _______________ (experience) the world through the words of another culture. I _______________ (learn) different ways of communicating and can use these new methods in my writing in Japanese.

13 14 15 16

Focus on Testing

Checking for Correct Tense

Activities 1, 2, and 3 in this section give you a lot of practice with verb tenses. When you are writing a paragraph under pressure in a testing situation, take time to make sure each verb form is in the correct tense. After you've finished writing, reread your paragraph from the beginning. First, make sure the overall time frame is correct; for example, if you're talking about a past event, most verbs in the paragraph should be in some form of the past. Then, locate the verb in each sentence. Is it in the correct form? Also, look for time expressions in each sentence (such as *since* or *for*) that might require a particular tense.

Timed Activity: 5 Minutes

Give yourself five minutes to look for and correct tense mistakes in the following paragraph. Read the whole paragraph before you make changes. Do not look up any information.

My life was very easy until I was fifteen years old. My family was rich and I never worry about anything. Then one day my father left us. We sell our beautiful house and moved to a small apartment. My mother has to go to work in an office. My brothers and sisters and I have left private school and began attending public school. I was extremely lonely and unhappy. I couldn't make friends at the new school. Everyone thought I was a snob. My life has changed when I got an after school job at a small bakery in town. The owner, Mrs. Garcia, took a special interest in me. She has taught me all about baking, running a small business and life. Two years ago, Mrs. Garcia retired. Since that time, I have been running the bakery on my own. It hasn't been easy to run a business and attend school part-time. I've had to work very hard but it has been worth it. I can truthfully say that I've been experiencing an easy life and a hard life and, in many ways, the hard life is better.

Using Demonstratives to Unify a Paragraph

A good writer uses phrases with *this, that, these,* or *those*—demonstratives—to refer to ideas in previous sentences.

> When I was fifteen, I read a book about Sammy Sosa. *That* was the first time I thought about becoming a professional baseball player.
>
> My grandmother went with me to the airport. She told me to work hard and not to forget my family. *Those* were her last words to me. I never saw her again.

4 Underline the phrases with demonstratives in Activity 3 on pages 63 and 64. What words or ideas do they refer to?

5 Complete these sentences with *this, that, these,* or *those.* Use *this* or *these* to refer to ideas or events in the present or recent past. Use *that* or *those* to refer to ideas or events farther in the past.

1. I first began to play soccer when I was four years old, and I have spent some of my happiest moments since ____________ time on the soccer field.
2. A very important holiday in China is New Year's. On ____________ day, we have a big feast.
3. My favorite aunt died recently. ____________ experience was sad and frightening because no one close to me had ever died before. However, it has made me see life differently.
4. I have learned French, Hungarian, and Spanish, and I'm now learning English. I love the different qualities of each of ____________ languages.

6 Prepositional phrases with demonstratives often appear at the beginning of sentences to unify a paragraph. Add one of the following phrases to the second sentence in each of the numbered items. Use a demonstrative *(this, that, these, those)* in each phrase.

for _________ reason	in _________ school
on _________ day	because of _________ factors
in _________ city	during _________ years

1. Two years and six months ago, my first child was born. My life changed.
   For this reason, my life changed.
   ____

2. I lived in a refugee camp in Thailand from the age of seven to eleven. My parents' only hope was going to live in North America.

____

3. I have always been shy. Learning a new language is a challenge for me.

____

4. I came to Mexico City two years ago. I have had many new experiences.

____

5. However, I was too short and was not thin enough. I could not continue to dance professionally.

____

6. I came to the International English Program six months ago. I have made many new friends.

____

Writing the First Draft

7 Write your paragraph about your personal accomplishment. You can use the ideas you wrote in the beginning of the chapter if you wish, as well as your topic sentence and concluding sentence. You can also use the demonstratives *this, that, these,* and *those* to unify your paragraph. Write on every other line so you can revise your paragraph easily.

PART 3 Edit and Revise

Editing Practice

Omitting Unimportant Ideas

1 Read the following paragraph. The writer has a lot of good ideas, but some of the ideas aren't important or don't give new information. Cross out the information she should leave out. If possible, combine repetitive ideas to make the paragraph shorter.

I have been taking an English class for the last six months. This has meant a rewarding but difficult change in my life. Before that I spent all my time raising my family, a daughter who is now five and a son who is three. My daughter's name is Karen. She is in kindergarten and my son now goes to day-care. Because I did not speak much English, my focus was my home and my neighborhood, where I felt comfortable and could speak Spanish. I spoke only Spanish

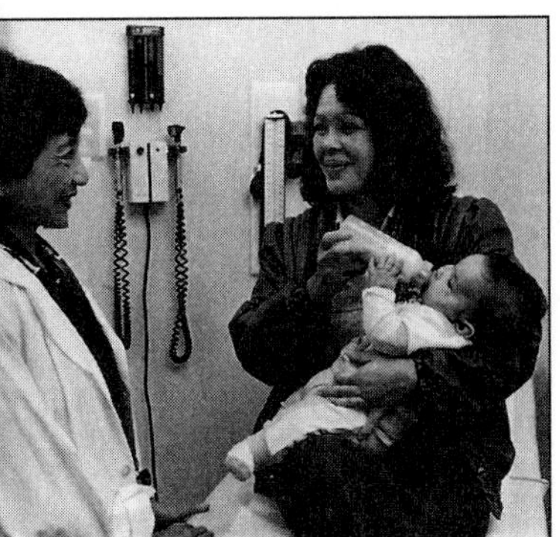

at home and in my neighborhood. When I needed to take my children to the doctor or speak with my landlord, my younger sisters translated for me. One of them would go with me and speak to the doctor in English and then tell me what he said in Spanish. Now I have become more independent. I have learned a lot from my classmates and I have also realized that as a mother I have had many experiences that they are interested in. Now my sisters tell me to speak to the doctor or landlord myself. I go to stores where I have to speak English and I speak English in the clinic where I take my son to the doctor. This was very difficult at first, but I have been feeling more and more comfortable about my ability to communicate with other English speakers. I hope to use this new confidence to get a job.

Using Correct Capitalization

2 Review the rules for capitalization in Appendix 2. Correct the capitalization in these sentences if necessary.

1. Because my Mother doesn't speak english, I have to translate for her.
2. When I first moved to the southwest, I got a job as a Salesperson.
3. I have lived in miami, Los Angeles, and dallas.
4. I received a Scholarship from Grant college in the Spring and started classes in september.
5. This semester I am taking Math, physics, english, and Government.

Using Correct Verb Forms

3 All the underlined words and phrases in the following paragraph contain errors. Correct the mistakes.

I <u>have been worked</u> (1) since <u>I have been young</u> (2), and I like to work. I <u>have been</u> (3) very good in mathematics, so when I <u>was having</u> (4) fifteen, I <u>start</u> (5) a tutoring business. Every afternoon after school I <u>am teaching</u> (6) math to younger children. I had fun and the students did too. That experience <u>has given</u> (7) me confidence. In 2001, I <u>have entered</u> (8) the university and started another business. I <u>taught</u> (9) business people how to use the Internet. This business <u>was being</u> (10) very successful. I <u>am spending</u> (11) all of my free time in my business. The first year, I failed three classes. This showed me that you can't do everything alone. Now I <u>have hire</u> (12) two assistants. My business is doing well and my classes <u>is</u> (13) too.

Editing Your Writing

4 Edit your paragraph using the following checklist. First, check your paragraph for content, organization, cohesion, and style, using items 1, 2, and 3 in the checklist. Then edit your paragraph for grammar and form, using items 4 and 5.

Editing Checklist

1. Content
   a. Does your paragraph describe your best qualities?
   b. Does it show that you can be successful in what you do?
   c. Does it let the reader infer what your best qualities are?
2. Organization
   a. Do you have too many ideas for one paragraph? Should you divide your paragraph into two paragraphs?
   b. Are there any ideas not relevant to the topic?
   c. Is your topic sentence positive? Does it make the reader want to find out more about you?
   d. Does each sentence add a new idea? Should you take out or combine repetitive sentences?
   e. Does your concluding sentence tell something you've learned or something you hope for in the future?
3. Cohesion and Style
   a. Have you used verb tenses correctly?
   b. Can you add demonstratives (*this, that, these, those*) and prepositional phrases with demonstratives to unify your paragraph?
4. Grammar
   a. Are your verb forms correct?
   b. Have you used run-on sentences or sentence fragments?
   c. Have you used plural and singular demonstratives correctly?
5. Form
   a. Is your capitalization correct?
   b. Is your spelling of past participles correct?

Peer Editing

5 Exchange papers with a classmate and edit each other's paragraphs. Circle or underline in pencil any words, phrases, or sentences that you don't understand or that you think need to be corrected. Then return your paragraphs. Discuss any questions you have with your partner.

Writing the Second Draft

6 After you edit your paragraph, rewrite it neatly, using correct form.

PART 4

A Step Beyond

Expansion Activities

1 Pretend to interview another student for a job or school. First find out what school or job she or he would like to apply for. Read her or his reply and ask for more information about the accomplishment. Then ask other questions, such as the following:

1. Why did you choose your major field of study?
2. What subjects in school have you liked the most/least? Why?
3. Tell me about your duties in past jobs.
4. Have you ever done any volunteer work? What kind and why?
5. Why are you interested in this position/school?
6. Where do you see yourself in five years?

2 Answer these questions about your writing:

1. What have you learned so far in this course?
2. How do you feel about writing?
3. What do you like most about writing?
4. What do you like least about writing?

3 Look in your school or city library for instructions on how to complete job and college applications. Following the instructions, fill out a sample application and have your classmates or teacher check it. Pay special attention to spelling, neat handwriting, and capitalization. Follow all directions carefully.

4 Some applications ask for an autobiography or a personal history. Expand the paragraph you wrote for this section into an autobiography. Don't just list events in your life. Explain why they were important and what you learned from them. Finish the autobiography with a paragraph describing your future goals.

Journal Writing

5 Write in your journal about one or more of these topics.

1. Write about a person you respect. Write about the qualities or experiences of that person that make you respect him or her.
2. List some of your classmates' names. Try to think of an adjective describing a classmate that begins with the same letter as his or her name, for example: trustworthy Tuan, assertive Abu, wonderful Wan.
3. Write about a job you'd love to have.

Video Activities: I Love My Job

Before You Watch. Discuss these questions in a group.

1. Have you ever had a job? If you did, did you like it? If you have had many jobs, which one was your favorite? Why?
2. Describe your ideal job. Why does this kind of job appeal to you?
3. Do you know anyone who is retired? What are the advantages and disadvantages of being retired?

Watch. Watch the video one time. Then discuss the following questions with your classmates.

1. Describe Lu. What does she look like? How old is she, probably?
2. Why do customers love Lu?
3. How does Lu feel about her job?
4. What kind of restaurant is Nicolosi's, probably?

Watch Again. Write answers to the following questions.

1. What skills does Lu have that make her good at her job?
2. What does it mean to "kill people with kindness"?
3. Have you ever known a wonderful waiter or waitress like Lu?
4. Why do you think Lu is still working?

After You Watch. You have been eating lunch at Nicolosi's restaurant for several years. Lu is your favorite waitress. Next week is Lu's 75th birthday, and you want to send her a birthday card. What will it say? Take out a piece of paper and use the form below to make a card for her. Start with the greeting below. Then add your own thoughts or good wishes, and sign your name.

Dear Lu,

Happy Birthday! ____

____

____

____

____________________,

____

Chapter 5

Lifestyles Around the World

IN THIS CHAPTER

You will write an anecdote, a short description of an experience that taught you a lesson.

PART 1

Before You Write

Exploring Ideas

Discussing Lessons People Learn from Experience

1 Read the following list of "lessons"—things that people might learn from experience. In small groups, discuss the list. Do you agree with all of the lessons? Try to think of experiences that might teach someone each of the lessons.

It's important to think for yourself.
Self-discipline is an essential quality.
Sometimes you have to take risks in order to get something you want.
Friendship is one of the most valuable things in life.
You should never make promises you can't keep.
If you want a good relationship, you have to compromise.
Sometimes parents really do know best.
Sometimes it's best to lie to the people you love.
Hard work can be satisfying.
The only thing that's certain is change.
It's great to be independent.

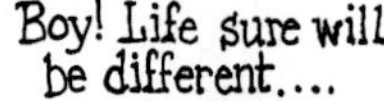

2 Make up a story for one of the pictures to show how the experience taught a lesson.

3 Think of an experience that taught you a lesson and write about it. The lesson might be one from the list in Activity 1 be another lesson. Write the lesson in a sentence at the top of a piece of paper and draw a line under it. Then write for ten minutes about the experience that taught you that lesson. Don't worry about correctness or organization now.

What Do You Think?

Analyzing the Moral of a Story

Analyzing the moral—or lesson—of a story is a useful critical thinking skill. Practice this skill with a partner. Take turns telling a story. It can be a fairy tale, a fable, a children's story, or a story from religious literature. Don't tell the moral of the tale—let your partner guess. When you have finished, talk about how the story teaches a lesson by answering these questions:

Who is the main character?
What is he or she like?
What happens to the main character?
Does he or she change? How?

Building Vocabulary

4 Work in small groups to complete the following chart with related forms of the words in the list. Use a dictionary to help you.

Nouns	Verbs	Adjectives
decision	______	______
importance		______
friendship		______
promise	______	
______	risk	______
______	change	
______		independent
______	______	valuable
______	lie	
______	compromise	
(self) discipline	______	______

5 Add other new words that you learned in your discussion or used in your writing.

Organizing Ideas

Understanding Anecdotes

An anecdote is a short description of something that really happened. Writers use anecdotes to illustrate or explain ideas. Many anecdotes or stories do not have topic sentences because they are organized chronologically rather than according to topic.

You are going to write an anecdote about something that happened to you that taught you a lesson about life. Your anecdote should answer these questions:

1. *When* and *where* did the story take place?
2. *Who* was involved and *what* was their relationship?
3. *What* happened?
4. *Why* did it happen?
5. *What* was the result?

6 Read the anecdote that follows and discuss it with your classmates. Does it answer all of the preceding questions? Which questions does most of the story answer? Which questions does it answer in the first two sentences? Which does it answer in the last sentence?

One summer weekend some friends and I decided to walk to a waterfall we had heard about. Since it was too far to walk along the road, we followed a railroad line. We had walked five or six miles when we came to a high rock wall where the tracks entered a tunnel. This tunnel didn't look very long, but it was narrow and we knew it would be dangerous if a train came. However, we couldn't climb the rocks or walk around them and no one wanted to go back. Finally we decided to go through. I knew it was foolish, but I went because the others did.

As soon as we entered the tunnel, we saw that it was longer and darker than we had thought. Suddenly everyone was frightened and we all began to run. "This is crazy!" I thought. We ran faster and it got lighter in the tunnel. Then we were outside and we fell on the ground gasping. About a minute later a train came through. That was when I finally realized the importance of thinking for myself.

Focus on Testing

Checking for Chronological Order

As you've just seen, an important part of writing an anecdote is organizing events in chronological order. When you write an anecdote in a timed testing situation, plan before you write. Start by listing the events in your story on a piece of scratch paper. Then check your list: Is everything in the right order? Is the order logical? If not, move things around or delete them. Are there any gaps? If so, fill in any missing information. Then use your list to write the paragraph.

Timed Activity: 5 Minutes

Think of a story that you know or an anecdote about your own life. Make notes of the events in order. Then tell the story to a classmate. Does he or she think that the events are in logical order?

Writing Anecdotes

When writing an anecdote, you might begin a new paragraph for several different reasons. Here are some of them:

1. The time or place of the story changes.
2. You begin to tell about a new person.
3. Something important happens in the story.
4. You stop telling the story and explain something about it.

7 In the anecdote about the tunnel, what was the writer's reason for starting a new paragraph when he wrote "As soon as we entered the tunnel . . ."?

Using Details

Your anecdote will be more interesting if you can make the reader "live" the experience with you. One way to do this is by using details to help the reader see what you saw and feel what you felt. Here is the second paragraph of the tunnel anecdote without the details that make it seem more real. What details did the writer leave out?

> We started to walk through the tunnel, but then we got frightened and started to run. After we got outside a train came through. That was when I finally realized the importance of thinking for myself.

One difficulty with details is that they can easily become *digressions:*

> One summer weekend some friends and I decided to walk to a waterfall we had heard about. This waterfall was called Horsetail Falls because it looked like a horse's tail. There was a place to swim at the bottom and it was a wonderful place for a picnic . . .

In a good anecdote, everything leads to the conclusion. If a detail leads away from the lesson (even if it is true and interesting), take it out of your anecdote.

8 Here are the writer's notes for part of the tunnel anecdote. In small groups, discuss the questions that follow.

didn't look very long
narrow, dangerous
rocks 80–100 ft. high—
couldn't climb them
river on left

a lot of bushes, more rocks
on right
couldn't go right or left
no trains all day—maybe
tracks not used?

1. Which details did the writer leave out of the anecdote?
2. Do you agree with his decisions?

PART 2

Write

Developing Cohesion and Style

Using the Past Perfect Tense

In the anecdote about the tunnel, everything happened in the past. The writer used mainly simple past tense verbs to tell the story in the order that it happened. But three times the writer looked back in time and used the past perfect tense to write about events that had happened earlier. This is one of the uses of the past perfect. It shows which action in the past happened first.

Examples

I *had* already *left* by the time he got back.
We *hadn't gone* one mile when the car broke down.

1 Find the three sentences in the anecdote that used the past perfect tense. Parts of these sentences are listed under 1, 2, and 3 in the following chart. What event happened *earlier* in each sentence? What happened *later*? Complete the chart.

In the Anecdote	Happened Earlier	Happened Later
1. We decided ________ to walk to a waterfall we ________ about.		We decided to walk to a waterfall.
2. We ________ five or six miles when we ________ to a high rock wall.		
3. We ________ that it was longer and darker than we ________.		

2 The following passage is an early draft of the tunnel anecdote. (You will notice that it still has a lot of digressions.) Fill in the blanks with the simple past tense or the past perfect tense of the verbs in parentheses.

One summer weekend some friends and I decided to take a picnic to a waterfall we had heard about. Some people drove (1) (drive) cars and ________ (2) (take) the food, but the rest of us ________ (3) (want) to walk. Since it was too far to walk along the road, we followed a railroad line. We had walked five or six miles when we came to a high rock wall where the tracks entered a tunnel. We ________ (4) (be) surprised. Nobody ________ (5) (tell) us about it. The tunnel didn't look very long, but it was narrow and we knew it would be dangerous if a train came. However, we couldn't climb the rocks or go around them, and no one wanted to go back. I ________ (6) (have) a good breakfast, but some of the others ________ (7) (not eat). They ________ (8) (want) to get to the waterfall and have lunch. Finally we decided to go through. I knew it was foolish, but I went because the others did.

As soon as we entered the tunnel, we saw that it was longer and darker than had thought. Earlier we _______________ (decide) to walk and to stay together, but suddenly everyone was frightened and we all began to run. "This is crazy," I thought. "Why didn't I go back?" We ran faster and it got lighter in the tunnel. Then we were outside and we fell on the ground gasping. No one _______________ (fall) in the tunnel. We _______________ (be) all safe. About a minute later a train came through.

9 10 11

We _______________ (be) upset because we _______________ (come) so close to death. We _______________ (be) also angry with ourselves for being so foolish. Later we _______________ (hear) that two boys _______________ (die) in that tunnel the month before. That was when I finally realized the importance of thinking for myself.

12 13 14 15 16

3 Reread the preceding paragraph and decide which sections are digressions and should be omitted. Cross them out.

Writing the First Draft

4 Now you are ready to write your own anecdote. Use the experience you wrote about earlier or choose another experience. Be sure to choose one that taught you a clear lesson. Write on every other line so you can revise your paragraph easily.

PART 3 Edit and Revise

Editing Practice

Omitting Digressions and Unimportant Details

1 The following paragraph is the first part of an anecdote. The last sentence of the anecdote will be "That was when I learned the satisfaction of doing hard work well." Revise the paragraph by taking out digressions and details that do not lead to the lesson of the anecdote. Use one line to cross them out. (You don't have to fix the grammar after you do this.)

The year I was fifteen my parents sent me to work on my uncle's farm for the summer. It was in South Carolina and they had peach trees, and cows and chickens. They didn't make much money and my father was always telling my uncle to sell the farm and come to Chicago. I didn't want to go and I didn't like it when I got there. It was very hot and muggy most of the time. My cousins got up at 4:30 in the morning and went to bed at 9:00 at night and in between they worked. I had never worked on a farm before, and my cousin Wayne had to teach me everything, like milking the cows, driving the tractor, and so on. We were the same age, but I was bigger than he was. I was already six feet tall. Even so I couldn't do anything as well as he could. I had a lot of friends at home and we always hung around together, especially in summer. I used to think about them. "They don't have to work on some dumb farm," I thought. "Why do I have to?"

2 Compare your revision to your classmates' work. Did you take out the same things? The following paragraph is a continuation of the story. Correct the underlined verbs if they are wrong.

<u>I'm</u> there about two weeks when Wayne and I <u>have</u> to load some bales of hay. After half an hour we <u>loaded</u> a lot of bales and it was getting hard to throw them up onto the wagon. "I'm going to miss the next one," I thought. But Wayne missed first. His bale <u>didn't go</u> high enough and it <u>has fallen</u> back down. I took a deep breath and <u>throw</u> mine. I did it! "Hey Dad!" Wayne called. "Did you see that?" I did it again and they <u>cheer</u>. I felt wonderful. After that everything <u>change</u>.

Wayne and I were friends and we enjoy competing with each other in everything. Usually he was better, but sometimes I am. I worked hard all summer and I love it. I learn a lot that summer, but the most important lesson is that day in the hayfield. That was when I learn the satisfaction of doing hard work well.

Editing Your Writing

3 Edit your anecdote using the following checklist. First, check your paragraph for content, organization, cohesion, and style, using items 1, 2, and 3 in the checklist. Then edit your paragraph for grammar and form, using items 4 and 5.

Editing Checklist

1. Content
   a. Is your story interesting?
   b. Does the lesson (conclusion) fit the story you told?
   c. Have you given enough information?
2. Organization
   a. Have you avoided unimportant details and digressions?
   b. Have you used paragraph divisions to make the story clearer?
3. Cohesion and Style
   a. Have you used transition words correctly?
   b. Are your sentences in logical order?
4. Grammar
   Have you used the past, present perfect, and past perfect tenses correctly?
5. Form
   a. Did you use correct paragraph format? (indentation, division of words between syllables, margins)
   b. Did you use correct punctuation? (capitalization, commas, periods)
   c. Did you check the spelling of the words you are not sure of?

Peer Editing

4 Exchange papers with a classmate and edit each other's anecdo line in pencil any words, phrases, or sentences that you don't unders think need to be corrected. Then return your anecdotes. Discuss any q have with your partner.

Writing the Second Draft

5 After you edit your anecdote, rewrite it neatly, using correct form. Give your anecdote to your teacher for comments.

PART 4 A Step Beyond

Expansion Activities

1 Read the anecdotes of two of your classmates. Then answer these questions about each anecdote.

1. What exactly made the anecdote interesting for you? Be specific. You can mention the incidents, some of the details, the lesson, or something else.
2. Do you agree with the student's conclusion (lesson) or not? Briefly explain why or why not.

2 Write down the story you discussed in the *What Do You Think?* box on page 73 (or you can write another story that teaches a lesson or has a moral). Be sure to include the moral of the story at the end. Form small groups, and read each other's stories. Are any of the stories similar? If your group has students from different countries, are there similar stories in those countries? Which story was the most interesting? Why? If you like, collect all the stories and make copies for all your classmates to read.

Journal Writing

3 Write in your journal about one or more of the following topics.

1. Write about a frustrating day or experience you've had recently.
2. Write about a change that has taken place in your life recently.
3. Write about a good time that you have had recently.

Video Activities: Telecommuting

Before You Watch. Discuss the following questions with your class or in groups.

1. Is traffic a problem in your area?
2. What can people in your area do to avoid sitting in traffic on the way to work?
3. Are businesses in your area doing anything to help workers who have to travel a long time to get to work?

Watch. Discuss the following questions with your classmates.

1. How does David Carroll reduce his commuting time?
2. Where does Marty Barrazo work?

Watch Again. Read the statements below. Say if they are true (T) or false (F). Then watch the video again and check your answers.

1. _____ David Carroll spends an hour commuting to work.
2. _____ David's company allows flexible work hours.
3. _____ Marty Barrazo works for an Internet company.
4. _____ He commutes three hours a day to the community computer center.
5. _____ Many people don't know that the community computer center exists.
6. _____ The computer center has very modern computers.
7. _____ Marty Barrazo is always grumpy when he gets home.

After You Watch. "Memo" means "memorandum." It is a kind of written communication between workers in an office, such as people in different departments or an employee and a boss.

Imagine you work for a large company. Your work hours are 8 A.M. to 5 P.M. You, and many employees like you, spend more than two hours a day commuting to and from work. Write a memo to your boss asking him to allow you to work flexible hours ("flextime"). Try to convince your boss by listing the advantages to the company. For example, workers will be less tired if they don't have to get up early and fight the traffic.

If you like, you may write this memo in small groups and have all the "employees" in the group sign their name.

Chapter 6

Global Connections

IN THIS CHAPTER

You are going to write a paragraph about the effects of globalization on your life.

PART 1

Before You Write

Exploring Ideas

Marshall McLuhan (1911–1980) was a Canadian professor and writer interested in modern communications. In his 1967 book *Understanding Media,* McLuhan wrote that "the new electronic interdependence recreates the world in the image of the global village." At that time, McLuhan was referring to how television allowed people all over the world to share information. With the introduction of new technologies such as satellite dishes, the Internet, and e-mail, McLuhan's idea of the "global village" seems more true now than ever.

Marshall McLuhan

Expanding a Definition

1 What does the phrase *global village* mean to you? Discuss it in small groups. Look at the following pictures. Can you think of another example of the global village?

Building Vocabulary

2 Here are some words that you may be able to use in your writing. Did you use any others in your discussion? If so, add them to the list.

Adjectives	Nouns	Verbs
isolated	multiculturalism	import
cosmopolitan	resources	export
multinational	diversity	influence
transnational	telecommunications	
technological	market	
	immigrant	
	tourism	

3 Work in small groups to complete this word forms chart. Use a dictionary to help you.

Noun	Verb	Adjective
________	________	isolated
diversity	________	________
immigrant	________	
tourism	________	________
________		technological
________	influence	________

4 Some long words are formed with several prefixes and suffixes. Prefixes generally change the meaning of a root word, and suffixes change a word's part of speech. Look at these words. How did the suffixes and prefixes change them? Use a dictionary to help you.

1. multiculturalism

Root			New Word	Change
culture	+ al	=	cultural	changes a noun to an adjective
	+ multi	=	________	________
	+ ism	=	________	________

2. immigration

Root			New Word	Change
migrate	+ ion	=	________	________
	+ im	=	________	________

3. telecommunication

Root			New Word	Change
communicate	+ tion	=	______________	______________
	+ tele	=	______________	______________

4. transnational

Root			New Word	Change
nation	+ al	=	______________	______________
	+ trans	=	______________	______________

What Do You Think?

Defining Terms

It's important to define certain terms when you use them in a discussion or essay because they can mean different things to different people. One way to define a word is to give an example. Practice this by reading the following words. Work with a partner, and take turns defining each one by giving an example. (You can look them up in the dictionary, but be prepared to explain what they mean to *you,* in your own words, because this is what you will have to do in a discussion or in writing.)

multiculturalism   diversity   global village   interdependence

Organizing Ideas

Listing Information

5 You are going to write about how the shrinking world affects your everyday life. Think about the good and bad effects of the global village. In the following chart, list them in the proper columns.

Good Effects	Bad Effects
______________	______________
______________	______________
______________	______________
______________	______________
______________	______________
______________	______________

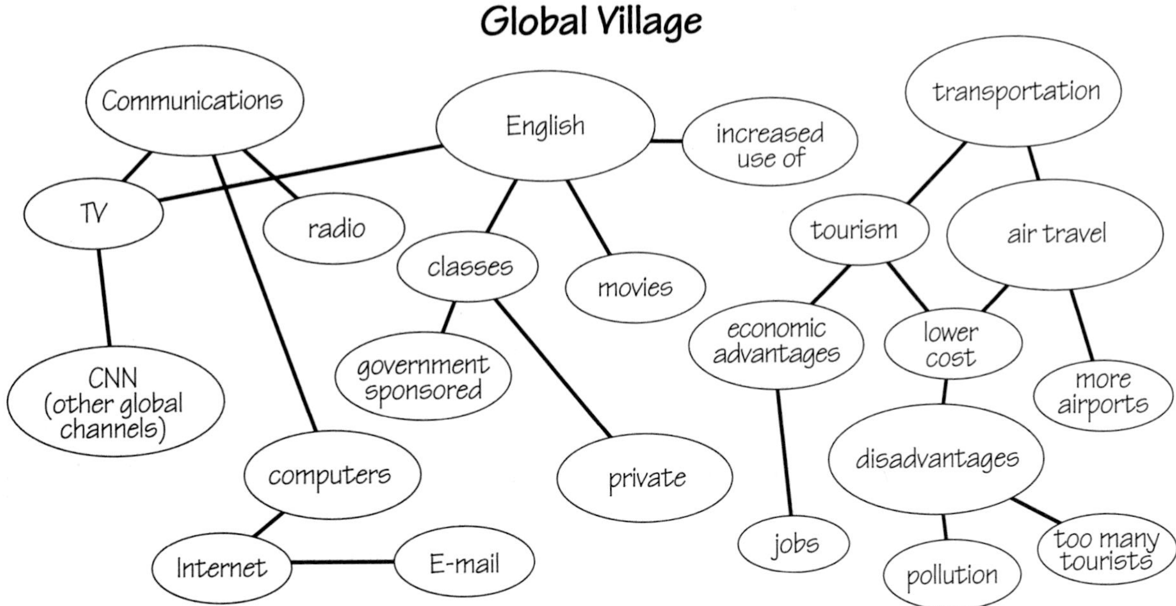

Clustering

> Clustering is one way to help you organize your ideas. It can help you decide what to focus on when a topic is very broad. To make a cluster diagram, write the topic on a piece of paper. Then write all your ideas about the topic around the paper. Connect the ideas that are related (go together). Look at the example above.

6 Make your own cluster diagram. First, get all of your ideas down on paper. Then, see which ideas are related and connect them.

7 Look at your cluster diagram and think about which ideas would make a good paragraph. Draw a circle around the part of the diagram (group of ideas) you want to write about. Use these questions to help you decide which ideas to choose.

- Is the information interesting?
- Are the different ideas clearly related?
- Do you have enough information for a paragraph?
- Can you limit the information to one paragraph?

Focus on Testing

Diagramming Your Ideas

In Organizing Ideas, you practiced clustering. This, and other kinds of diagrams can help you save time when you are writing under pressure. Take a few minutes *before* you start writing in a testing situation to diagram your ideas. You can draw a cluster, or any other kind of diagram, such as a flow chart, that works for you. This will help you organize your ideas and see how they are related before you write.

Timed Activity: 5 Minutes

Give yourself five minutes to draw a diagram listing the effects of cars on modern life. After you are finished, compare your work with your classmates' work. Are there any important ideas that you left out?

PART 2 Write

Developing Cohesion and Style

Choosing the Correct Part of Speech

When you write a paragraph or longer composition, be careful to use the correct forms of words that have different forms for different parts of speech.

Examples

I have an appointment for a medical *examination* today.
The doctor *examined* the young boy.
The medical *examiner* said that the man had died from a heart attack.

1 Complete each sentence with the correct part of speech of the word in parentheses.

1. Many countries are worried about increasing ________________ (immigrate) and have strict laws to control the number of people who can become citizens.

2. ________________ (tourist) is an important source of revenue for a lot of countries.

3. Many cities in the United States have a _______________ (multiculturalism) atmosphere. This can easily be seen in the great _______________ (diverse) of ethnic restaurants.

4. The world is truly becoming _______________ (interdependence). No country today can survive in _______________ (isolate).

5. Laws that limit the _______________ (import) of certain products are necessary to help local industries grow.

6. It is almost impossible to keep up with all the recent _______________ (technology) changes.

Using Restrictive Relative Clauses

The relative pronouns *who, which, where,* and *that* can be used to introduce restrictive relative clauses. The restrictive relative clauses are underlined in the following examples.

Examples	**Notes**
The woman *who/that* runs the restaurant is Japanese.	*Who* refers to people.
The watch *that/which* I bought you is Swiss.	*Which* refers to things. *That* refers to people and things.
The office *where* I work employs people from four different countries.	*Where* refers to places.

2 Complete the following sentences with the correct relative pronouns.

1. The global village has arrived, and people _______________ do not realize this are going to be left behind.

2. The use of computers, _______________ now link not only governments but individuals all over the world, has broken down national borders.

3. The global village is a place _______________ many languages are spoken; however, the one _______________ is predominant is English.

4. Parts for the car ______________ I just bought were made in six different countries.

5. Some futurists foresee the world as city-states ______________ are connected by technology.

Using Specific Examples

Your writing will be more interesting if you use specific examples to support your statements.

Example

I have found things to like in every country I have visited. The food and the shopping in Singapore was incredible. I loved the stark beauty of the countryside in Oman. I enjoyed the warm and friendly people in Mexico.

3 Read these two paragraphs. Then work with a partner and answer these questions about the paragraphs. Which one is more interesting? Why?

1. People often say that the world is getting smaller, and I believe that this is true. However, it is not only getting smaller, it is becoming more homogenous. People are moving from place to place. In the small town where I live, you can eat in restaurants from several different countries. The neighborhood school has children from many different language backgrounds. We can watch television in different languages too. In addition, I drive a foreign car, have an imported television, VCR, and camera. Last of all, most of my clothes were made overseas.

2. This is a typical day in the "global village" where I live. My Japanese clock radio wakes me up. I dress in my T-shirt, which was made in Thailand, and my jeans, which were made in Taiwan. I walk out into a Spanish-named street full of German cars. I go for breakfast at a Mexican cafe run by a Japanese woman and then stop at the Korean grocery store. Back home, I can listen to the news in Spanish, Chinese, Japanese, Arabic, Korean, or Hindi. My wife's school has parent-teacher association meetings that look like a mini United Nations. Where is this multicultural paradise? In California, but it could be in many other places. The world is looking more and more like the United States, but the United States is also looking more and more like the rest of the world.

4 Look at your cluster diagram and the notes you made for your paragraph. Do you need more examples? Add them.

Writing the First Draft

5 Write your paragraph using the organization you worked out at the beginning of this chapter. Write on every other line so that you can revise your paragraph easily.

PART 3

Edit and Revise

Editing Practice

Punctuating Relative Clauses

There are two different types of relative clauses: restrictive and nonrestrictive.

- A restrictive relative clause tells you which person, place, or thing the writer is referring to. The information in the restrictive relative clause is necessary to complete the sentence. Don't use commas with restrictive clauses.

  Examples

  Children *who are bilingual* have an advantage over their monolingual playmates.

  May and October are the months that *I like best.*

Note that if you omit the restrictive relative clauses *who are bilingual* (example 1) and *that I like best* (example 2), the sentences are incomplete.

- A nonrestrictive relative clause gives additional information. This additional information is not necessary to complete the sentence. In nonrestrictive clauses, use *which* instead of *that* to refer to things. Use commas to separate a nonrestrictive clause from the rest of the sentence.

  Examples

  My brother's children, *who are bilingual,* are seven and ten years old.

  May and October, *which have the best weather,* are my favorite months.

Note that if you omit the nonrestrictive relative clauses *who are bilingual* (example 1) and *which have the best weather* (example 2), the sentences are still complete.

Do not use *that* with nonrestrictive relative clauses.

1 Read these sentences and add commas where necessary.

1. The global village which was first discussed by Marshall McLuhan in the 1960s has finally come to be.
2. The teachers who teach in the global village should have a multicultural point of view.
3. My father works in a cement factory that is owned by Japanese businessmen.
4. New technology which is the backbone of the global village is growing at a faster rate than ever.
5. My students who come from six different countries are very interested in learning about other places in the world.
6. World markets are controlled by huge corporations that may not care about their workers.

Editing Your Writing

2 Edit your paragraph, using the checklist provided here. First, check your paragraph for content, organization, cohesion, and style, using items 1, 2, and 3 in the checklist. Then edit your paragraph for grammar and form, using items 4 and 5.

Editing Checklist

1. Content
   Does your paragraph give specific examples when necessary?
2. Organization
   Does your paragraph have a narrow enough focus?
3. Cohesion and Style
   Have you used relative clauses correctly?
4. Grammar
   Have you used the correct part of speech for each word?
5. Form
   a. Have you used a capital letter to begin each sentence?
   b. Have you used a period to end each sentence?
   c. Have you punctuated relative clauses correctly?

Peer Editing

3 Exchange papers with another classmate and edit each other's paragraphs. Circle or underline in pencil any words, phrases, or sentences that you don't understand or that you think need to be corrected. Then return your paragraphs. Discuss any questions you have with your partner.

Writing the Second Draft

4 Rewrite your paragraph neatly, using correct form. Then give it to your teacher for comments.

PART 4

A Step Beyond

Expansion Activities

1 Find an article in a magazine or a newspaper that talks about the global village. Does the writer mention any effects that you and your classmates have not thought of?

2 Interview classmates and/or teachers about the global village. Compile their reactions and write a composition incorporating their opinions.

3 Interview an older friend or relative about how his/her world has changed in the past 30–40 years. Take notes. Then, in small groups, share your findings with other classmates.

4 Have you ever heard of a time capsule? A time capsule is a group of items that can tell people in the future something about the way people live today. Some people put such items in a box or other container, close the container, and put it away. They write instructions telling people not to open it for 100 years or more. Work in small groups. Brainstorm a list of items to put in a time capsule. They should be items that will best help people in the future understand what life is like now. Brainstorm a list of items. Then discuss them and choose *only* ten items for your capsule. When you finish, join another group and share your lists. How are your items similar? How are they different? Why did you choose these items?

Journal Writing

5 Write about one or both of the following topics.

1. Write about how you think your world will change in the next twenty years. Write for fifteen minutes.
2. Write about any aspect of the global village that interests you.

Video Activities: Teen Talk

Before You Watch. Discuss these questions in a group.

1. What are the most common problems that teenagers have?
2. How do teenagers get help when they have a problem?
3. If you have a problem, do you think it's easier to talk to a stranger or to someone you know?

Watch. Discuss the following questions in a group.

1. What is "Teen Talk"?

   a. a magazine b. a Website c. a school group

2. On Teen Talk, teenagers can . . . (Choose 2 answers)

   a. talk to other teens about their problems
   b. see advertisements for products they might like
   c. get help with homework
   d. learn about resources to help them with their problems

Watch Again. Fill in the answers.

1. List three examples of problems that the users of Teen Talk discuss.

   a. ______________________________
   b. ______________________________
   c. ______________________________

2. The teen girl believes that just ________________ about something can help teens to solve problems.
3. The "number 1 goal" of Teen Talk was to give teens a place to go to find ________________.

After You Watch. Imagine that you are one of the operators on Teen Talk. In other words, you are one of the adults that answers the teens' questions.

Imagine that you have received the following e-mail:

Hello,
My name is Tammy. I am 16 years old and I hope you can help me because I don't know what to do. I had a boyfriend for about three months but last week he told me he didn't love me anymore. Then I saw him with one of my best friends. I am so depressed. I feel like I have lost everything. I have no one to talk to. My parents don't understand anything and anyway, they're too busy working to pay attention to me. Please help me!

In small groups, talk about the advice you could give Tammy. Try to think of specific resources (people and places) that could help Tammy with her problem. Then write your answer.

Chapter 7

Language and Communication

IN THIS CHAPTER

You are going to write about someone's experiences living in a foreign country and trying to learn a new language.

PART 1

Before You Write

Exploring Ideas

Interviewing Someone

1 Many people move to other countries. In small groups, think about why they do this. List the reasons on the following lines.

2 Living in a foreign country can be very difficult, especially when you do not speak the language well. Discuss some of the problems that newcomers to your country might have. List them on the following lines.

3 For your essay, you are going to interview someone about his/her experiences living in a foreign country where he/she did not speak the language. Make a list of possible interview questions.

What Do You Think?

Distinguishing Appropriate Topics

When you interview someone to get information for a story, it's important to know which questions are appropriate—or polite—to ask, and which are not. Knowing this depends partly on how familiar you are with the person's culture, partly on common sense, and partly on the purpose or topic of the interview. Practice distinguishing appropriate from inappropriate interview questions. Work with a partner. Read the following list of questions. Decide which questions are appropriate, and which are inappropriate, to ask in an interview about a newcomer's experiences in your culture. Write "A" (appropriate) or "I" (inappropriate) next to each question. Then think of some additional appropriate questions.

_____ How old are you?

_____ When did you come to this country?

_____ Why don't you speak our language well?

_____ What do you do for a living?

_____ Why aren't you married?

_____ What religion are you?

_____ How much money do you make?

_____ Where did/do you go to school?

_____ What do you think of the government of this country?

_____ What's your favorite food?

_____ Why don't you have children?

4 Work in pairs. Interview your partner, using the interview questions you wrote for Activity 3. On a separate page, take notes on your partner's answers. Then your partner will interview you and take notes. When your partner interviews you, you may answer as yourself, or you may pretend you are someone you know or someone in the picture on page 95.

5 Exchange notes. What else can you add to the notes your partner made?

Building Vocabulary

6 In your discussion you may have heard some words you don't understand, or you may not know the English word for some of the ideas you want to express. Find out the meaning of any words you don't understand and add them to the following list.

Nouns	Verbs	Adjectives
confusion	confuse	anxious
depression	depress	confused
excitement	emigrate	depressed
homeland	excite	excited
humiliation	humiliate	homesick
native land	immigrate	humiliated
refugee	thrill	thrilled
thrill	______	upset
______	______	frightened
______	______	disappointed
______	______	surprised
______	______	______
______	______	______

7 Look at the adjectives above. Which ones describe pleasant feelings? Which ones describe unpleasant feelings?

Pleasant Feelings	Unpleasant Feelings
______	______
______	______
______	______
______	______
______	______

Using Verbal Adjectives to Describe Feelings

Many of the verbs that describe emotions are verbal adjectives. Verbal adjectives take two forms. One form ends in *-ed*. It describes the person (or animal) that has a feeling. The other form ends in *-ing*. It describes the person, animal, or thing that creates a feeling.

Examples

Eva heard some *surprising* news.

She was *surprised* by the news.

Here is a list of some common verbal adjectives:

confused	confusing	humiliated	humiliating
depressed	depressing	surprised	surprising
disappointed	disappointing	tired	tiring
excited	exciting	terrified	terrifying
frightened	frightening	thrilled	thrilling

8 Look at these sentences. Circle the noun or noun phrase that the adjective in italics describes.

1. At first, (not being able to understand the language) was *terrifying* to Ahmad.
2. Tran was *disappointed* when he couldn't find a job.
3. Living in a new country is *confusing* to most people.
4. Wilma was *surprised* that learning English was so easy.
5. Daoud was *thrilled* at winning the French prize.

9 Complete these sentences with adjective forms of the following words.

excite	tire	surprise
frighten	depress	

1. Tran was ____surprised____ by American customs.
2. Amara thought working full-time and studying was ________________.
3. Alain was ________________ and homesick when he first moved to the United States.
4. At first, Junko thought that life in New York was ________________ but later she got very lonely.
5. Some people think that flying is ________________.

10 Complete these sentences with verbal adjectives. Use verbal adjectives with the same meaning as *happy*, *sad*, or *scary*.

1. Life in a foreign country can be ________________.
2. I was ________________ on the first day of class.
3. Leaving home is ________________.
4. My friends and family were ________________ when I left.

11 Write some sentences for your paragraphs, using verbal adjectives.

Organizing Ideas

Keeping to One Subject

When you write, be careful to keep to the subject. All of the information that you give should be closely related to the topic of your paragraph.

12 Read this paragraph. Does it contain any irrelevant information? Cross out any sentences that do not belong.

When Lee Kim first arrived in the United States from Korea, he was very frightened. Suddenly, he was entering a world that was almost totally incomprehensible to him. He was living in an apartment. He was unable to obtain information he needed. Lee could not read a street sign, ask a question, or understand directions. Lee's brother spoke English well. However, Lee's life changed for the better when he decided to go to Newton Community College to take English classes. This school is located on the corner of Broad Street and First Avenue.

Focus on Testing

Developing Your Ideas

In Exploring Ideas, you practiced asking questions about a paragraph. This is a good technique to use when you have to write a paragraph for a timed test. After you write, take a few minutes to ask yourself *wh-* questions (*who*, *what*, *where*, *when*, *how*, etc.) about each sentence in your paragraph. If your sentences already answer each question, congratulations! You probably have a well-developed paragraph. If not, add sentences to develop your ideas further.

Timed Activity: 10 Minutes

Read the following paragraph. Ask yourself *wh-* questions to find out what information is missing. Use your imagination to add details to the paragraph. When you are finished, compare your paragraph with a classmate's. Did you both add the same types of information?

Marsha Foster was very excited when her company gave her a job in a foreign country. When she first arrived in the new country, her life was very difficult because she couldn't speak the language. Then, she took classes. Now she is very happy. She doesn't want to go back to her country.

Dividing a Composition into Paragraphs

Your story can have two or more paragraphs. For example, the first paragraph might be about the person's life upon first arriving and a second paragraph about how his or her life changed. Alternatively, you can write about the person's life before leaving his or her country and his or her life after having arrived.

13 Look at the notes you made for your story. Divide them into paragraphs. Is there any information that seems irrelevant? Is there any information you should add?

Writing Topic Sentences

A good topic sentence should capture the reader's interest and explain what the paragraph is about.

14 Look at these topic sentences. Which ones do you like? Why? Add information to the ones you don't like to make them more interesting. Remember that there are several ways to make good topic sentences.

1. Basima never cared about learning English before the summer of 1998.
2. Wai Fon Yu was born in Beijing.
3. John thought he spoke Spanish well until he moved to Venezuela.
4. Domingo is an immigrant from Spain.
5. His name is Walid.

15 Write a topic sentence for the first paragraph of your story.

Writing Concluding Sentences

Although most people who move to a new country face many problems, they usually have hope for the future. One way to conclude a story about a personal experience is with a sentence expressing that hope.

16 Look at these concluding sentences. Which ones do you like the best? Why?

1. Marta is looking forward to a better future now that she has learned to speak English well.
2. After two years in Japan, Shirley still can't even say hello to her neighbors.
3. Although Lou is still sometimes homesick, he knows that his decision to leave the United States was the right one.
4. Mohammed is waiting for the day when he can feel comfortable speaking English.

PART 2

Write

Developing Cohesion and Style

Using Gerunds as Subjects

A gerund is the *-ing* form of a verb used as a noun—for example, *moving, becoming, working*. (See Appendix 1 for rules for spelling changes.) Gerunds or gerund phrases are sometimes subjects of sentences.

Look at these sentences with gerund phrases.

Examples

Moving to the United States was the most exciting experience of Juan's life.

Being sent to live in Saudi Arabia made Joseph nervous.

Learning French was very difficult for Michael.

We make negative gerunds with the word *not*.

Not being able to read street signs was the hardest part of living in Turkey.

1 Make gerund phrases from the words in parentheses to write sentences in items 1–5 that follow.

1. (Talk about politics) was forbidden in Teresa's country

   Talking about politics was forbidden in Teresa's country.

2. (Learn to live in a new culture) is difficult for anyone

   ____

3. (Leave your homeland) is never easy

   ____

4. (Not be able to even order lunch) was humiliating for Gloria

   ____

5. (Not speak the language) made Jaime feel isolated

   ____

2 Complete these sentences with a gerund phrase.

1. Having a conversation in a foreign language for the first time is a thrilling experience.
2. ______________________ made Marta very happy.
3. ______________________ can be very tiring.
4. ______________________ is important to Yoko.
5. ______________________ was easy for Katrina.

Using Gerunds in Parallel Constructions

When you write, it is important to use gerunds in parallel constructions. The gerunds in the following sentences are parallel. The sentences are correct.

Examples

Working during the day and *studying* at night made Miguel very tired.

Speaking and *listening* to English all day gave me a headache.

The gerunds in these sentences are not parallel. The sentences are incorrect.

Examples

Visiting new places and *to meet* new people always interested Shadi.

Going to the movies and *watch* television helped Henry improve his Japanese.

3 The following paragraph includes some mistakes in the use of gerunds and infinitives. Find the mistakes and correct them.

Leaving friends and family is difficult.

A Difficult Decision

Deciding

~~Decide~~ to leave her country was very difficult for Berta. Unfortunately, in her native country she was unable to going to school or find a good job. When her husband suggested that they leave, she knew he was right. However, when she first arrived in the United States, she was very unhappy. Not being able to speak English well made it difficult for her to feel at home. In addition she and her husband hardly saw each other. Work during the day and going to school at night meant that there was little time for them to be together. That was five years ago. Now they both speak English and have good jobs. They also have a daughter and a son. Although to leave was not easy, Berta knows that she making the right decision.

Using Would *and* Used to

When English speakers talk about past events they often use the simple past tense. When they are talking about past habits, however, they sometimes use *would* + verb or *used to* + verb.

Examples

When I was young, I *used to* get up early every morning.

When I was young, I *would* get up early every morning.

You can use *would* and *used to* to talk about repeated activities. However, for continuing states using verbs such as *have, think, live, believe,* and *own* you can use *used to* only.

Examples

Her grandfather *used to* have a long white beard.

She *used to* think that he was the oldest man in the world.

Remember that you cannot use *would* and *used to* for activities that happened only once or twice or states that continued for only a short time. In these cases you must use the simple past tense.

Examples

Anna started school when she was seven.

On the first day of school she was afraid because she thought that her mother was leaving her forever.

4 Complete these sentences in as many ways as possible. Some sentences can take only the simple past. Others can take the simple past or *used to*. Some can take the simple past, *would,* or *used to.*

1. Marta ___used to___ (listen) to language tapes when she was on the bus.
2. When he was young, Alfonso ______________ (hate) studying English.
3. Jacob never ______________ (understand) what young children said.
4. When Greta was fifteen, she ______________ (come) to live in the United States.
5. In El Salvador, Teresa's family ______________ (own) a large farm.

Many times students use *used to* too often in one paragraph. Good writers often begin with a sentence using *used to* and then continue with *would* or the simple past tense.

5 Read this paragraph. Then discuss it with a partner. Do you like it? Say why or why not.

From the time he arrived in Beijing, Harry was obsessed with learning Chinese. He used to get up every morning before work and study for two hours. He used to listen to Chinese tapes in his car on his way to work. He used to ask everyone in the office to speak to him in Chinese even though he used to get very confused because he used to not understand what they said. At night, Harry used to take Chinese classes. On the weekends, he used to go to Chinese movies and listen to Chinese music. Unfortunately, he used to be lonely because he didn't used to have many friends.

6 Rewrite the paragraph, changing *used to* to *would* or the simple past tense to make it more interesting.

7 Think about the paragraphs you are going to write about a newcomer to your country. Write three or four sentences using *used to* or *would* that you could use in your composition.

Writing the First Draft

8 Write your composition using the topic sentence you wrote and the notes you made. Make your paragraphs interesting by adding details. Don't worry about grammar when you write the first draft. Write on every other line so you can revise your paragraph easily.

PART 3 Edit and Revise

Editing Practice

Adding Topic and Concluding Sentences and Omitting Irrelevant Information

1 The first paragraph of the following composition needs a topic sentence, and the last paragraph needs a concluding sentence. Read the story and then add a topic sentence and a concluding sentence. Cross out any irrelevant information.

____

________________________. When Maryam was very young she lived in a small village in Bosnia with her parents and her brothers and sisters. Her parents were farmers. They grew wheat and vegetables. At that time, there was a war in Bosnia. Sometimes her parents would talk about the war but only a few soldiers came to Maryam's village, so her family felt safe. Maryam's older brother decided not to fight in the war. Then one day bombs began to fall on their village and many soldiers came to fight there. Maryam's parents died in the fighting. Maryam and her sister went to live with their grandmother in the city of Sarajevo. Sarajevo used to be beautiful city but it was destroyed in the war. One day when Maryam was fourteen their grandmother came and told them that they were going to go to the United States to live with their aunt.

At first, Maryam's life in the United States was very difficult. She went to an American high school and she felt very uncomfortable there. She went to John F. Kennedy High School in Trenton, New Jersey. Learning English wasn't easy, and the other students were very different from her. Gradually, Maryam began to make friends, first with other foreign students and finally with some Americans. She learned to speak English well and became comfortable with the American way of life. Although Maryam still thought about her life in Bosnia, she didn't feel homesick anymore. Maryam's sister was still planning to return to Bosnia. Today Maryam is eighteen years old. When she graduates from high school, she plans to go to college to become a nurse. ____________________

____.

Punctuating Sentences with Transitions and Subordinating Conjunctions

Remember to use transition words to connect ideas in a paragraph. Don't overuse them, however. When transition words such as *first of all, finally, in addition,* and *also* come at the beginning of a sentence, put a comma after them.

Example

At first, Maryam's life in the United States was very difficult.

Don't confuse subordinating conjunctions such as *when* and *because* with transition words. (See Appendix 5 for lists of subordinating conjunctions and Appendix 6 for lists of transition words.) Subordinating conjunctions connect dependent clauses and independent clauses within a sentence. Transition words connect ideas within a paragraph, to make it cohesive.

Subordinating conjunction:	I was unhappy, *so* I wanted to go home.
Transition word:	I couldn't speak English. I had no friends, and I was living in a terrible place. *Therefore*, I wanted to go home.

2 Edit this paragraph for correct punctuation around transition words and subordinating conjunctions.

May 14, 1981 was the most memorable day in my life. On that day, my family left our home in Iran to go to live in the United States. Although I was only eight years old I thought I knew what life would be like in America. Because I had seen many movies about life there I remember wondering if I would be able to have a horse and carry a gun. In addition even though my father kept telling me that we were going to be living in a big city, I still imagined myself in the "Wild West."

Editing Your Writing

3 Edit your composition, using the following checklist. First, check your paragraph for content, organization, cohesion, and style, using items 1, 2, and 3 in the checklist. Then edit your paragraph for grammar and form, using items 4 and 5.

Editing Checklist

1. Content
   a. Is the information interesting?
   b. Does the composition answer most of the reader's questions?
2. Organization
   a. Are paragraphs organized chronologically?
   b. Does your first paragraph have a good topic sentence?
   c. Does your last paragraph have a concluding sentence?
3. Cohesion and Style
   a. Are your gerund constructions parallel?
   b. Did you use *used to* too often?
4. Grammar
   a. Did you use *used to* and *would* correctly?
   b. Did you use verbal adjectives correctly?
5. Form
   a. Did you use correct paragraph format? (indentation, division of words between syllables, margins)
   b. Did you use correct punctuation? (capitalization, commas, periods)
   c. Did you check the spelling of the words you are not sure of?

Peer Editing

4 Exchange papers with another classmate and edit each other's compositions. Circle or underline in pencil any words, phrases, or sentences that you don't understand or that you think need to be corrected. Then return your compositions. Discuss any questions you have with your partner.

Writing the Second Draft

5 After you edit your composition, rewrite it neatly, using correct form. Give your composition to your teacher for comments.

PART 4

A Step Beyond

Expansion Activities

1 Read your stories aloud in small groups. If you have written about yourself or someone from your country, you can bring in pictures of your family and your native country.

2 If you have never lived in a foreign country, write about your experiences learning and using English in your own country. Think about these questions. Have you ever tried to speak with a tourist using English? Were you able to understand each other? Have you watched movies or listened to music in English and tried to understand the words? Was it frustrating or challenging?

Journal Writing

3 Write in your journal for ten or fifteen minutes about one or both of the following topics.

1. Is it important to learn another language? Why or why not?
2. What are the difficulties in learning to speak a foreign language?

Video Activities: Technology for the Disabled

Before You Watch. Discuss the following in a group.

1. What are *disabilities*? Do you have a friend or a relative who is *disabled*?
2. Define these terms: paraplegic, quadriplegic.
3. What are some of the difficulties that disabled people have in an "abled" world?

Watch. Discuss the following questions in a group.

1. Guido Corona is blind. How does technology help him to see?
2. The man in the wheelchair cannot use his hands. How can he use a computer?
3. What percentage of Americans have a disability?

Watch Again. Read the questions below. Fill in the blanks. Then watch the video again to check your answers.

1. The IBM Home Page Reader allows _______________ people to access everything on the Web. It was created by a person with a _______________.
2. The man in the wheelchair is able to use a computer with the help of a device called Track 2000. With this program, the man can move the computer cursor by moving his _______________, and he can "right click" and "left click" a mouse by twitching his _______________.

After You Watch. Below is a list of famous people, living and dead, who accomplished great things even though they had a disability. Choose a name from the list. Use an encyclopedia or the Internet (search for "famous people with disabilities") to write a short biography of this person. Tell the facts of this person's life, and be sure to explain how this person succeeded in spite of his or her disability.

Andrea Bocelli	Franklin D. Roosevelt	Stevie Wonder
Chris Reeves	Tom Cruise	Walt Disney
Beethoven	Albert Einstein	Marlee Matlin
Van Gogh	Stephen Hawkins	Sarah Bernhardt
Ray Charles	Thomas Alva Edison	Winston Churchill
"Magic" Johnson	Robin Williams	

Chapter 8

Tastes and Preferences

IN THIS CHAPTER

You are going to write a composition comparing two types of housing.

PART 1 Before You Write

Exploring Ideas

1 As a class or in small groups, look at the following pictures. Discuss the types of living situations. How are they similar? How are they different? What kind(s) of living situation would you prefer? What kind(s) don't you like? Why?

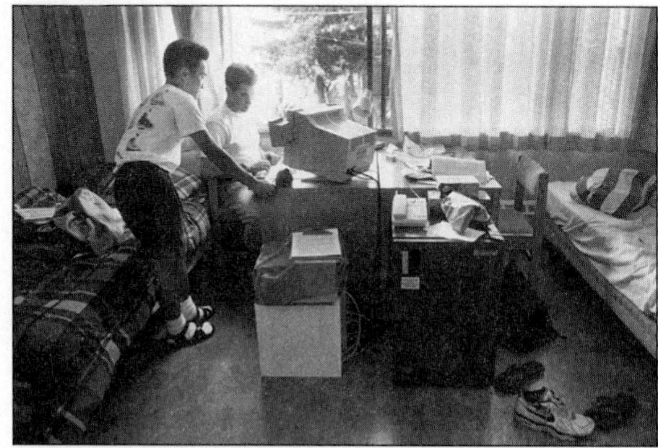

You are going to write a composition comparing two different types of student living situations. You will write about how they are similar and how they are different.

2 Work with a partner or in small groups. Take turns discussing different housing situations that students often live in. (Think about students who are studying in universities in their hometowns and students who are studying away from home.) Describe the advantages and disadvantages of each living situation. Ask questions and take notes. When you finish discussing them, choose two different kinds of housing to write about.

What Do You Think?

Finding a Basis of Comparison

You are going to write a comparison in this chapter. When you compare situations, places, things, or people, there must be a basis of comparison. That is, even though the items may be very different, they must have something basic in common. For example, although a rock musician and the pope both may be famous people, being famous is not enough of a basis of comparison. You might, however, compare the pope as a leader of a church to the president of the United States as a leader of a country.

Practice this by looking at the following list. With a partner, decide if each pair has enough similarities to compare them successfully:

1. the Nile River/New York City
2. a police officer/a coal miner
3. a baby/an old man
4. swimming/shopping
5. a tricycle/a pair of skis
6. bike riding/skiing
7. San Francisco/Tel Aviv
8. the Amazon River/the Mississippi River

---

3 Write about the two living situations that you chose. Write as much as you can about them in ten minutes.

4 As a class, discuss your notes from Activity 3 about the two types of housing. What characteristics can you compare? Discuss the following list of characteristics. Did you think of these characteristics? Did you think of other characteristics? Add them to the list.

privacy
expense
personal space
public space
responsibilities
rights

social life
access to university facilities
access to stores, etc.
safety
comfort

Building Vocabulary

5 Here are some words that you may be able to use in your comparisons. Did you use any others in the notes you wrote? If so, add them to the list.

Adjectives	Nouns	Verbs
accessible	roommate	share
inexpensive	housemate	divide
lonesome	companionship	concentrate
cozy	chores	
spacious	rooming house	
self-sufficient	landlady	
dependable	landlord	
exorbitant	utilities	
convenient	rent	
cheap	public transportation	
tidy	solitude	
orderly	dormitory (dorm)	
messy		
off-campus		
on-campus		

6 Look at the adjectives above. Use arrows to connect the opposites. Look at the adjectives that are left. Think of as many other opposites as you can. Write the pairs of words on the lines provided.

__________ __________ __________ __________

__________ __________ __________ __________

__________ __________ __________ __________

7 Look at the nouns, think about the parts of the words, and answer the questions. Use a dictionary to help you.

roommate housemate

1. What are the two parts of these words?
2. Can you guess the meaning of the second part?
3. Can you think of any other words that end in the second part?

landlady landlord

1. What are the two parts of these words?
2. What do the second parts of the words show?

companionship

1. What are the two parts of this word?
2. Can you think of any other words that end in the second part?

Organizing Ideas

Listing Similarities and Differences

8 Look at this example of some possible similarities and differences between living at home and living with another family.

Similarities	**Differences**
Both: not lonely	*at home*
less stressful	more comfortable and familiar
family support in an emergency	less expensive
	with another family
	little household responsibility
	more privacy

Make a list of the similarities and differences between the living situations you chose.

Similarities	**Differences**
Both: ____________	Living situation A: ____________
____________	____________
____________	____________
____________	____________
____________	Living situation B: ____________
____________	____________
____________	____________
____________	____________

9 Look at the two lists. Decide whether there are more similarities or differences between the situations you chose. If there are more similarities, you should focus on the similarities in your composition, although you will also have to mention the differences. If there are more differences, you should focus on them.

10 Read this composition comparing renting a room with a family and living with your own family. Does the composition focus more on similarities or differences?

Family Living

Living at home or renting a room in another family's house both have some important benefits for students. Of course, these two situations have their differences. Living at home is less expensive and it is usually more comfortable to live with people you know. On the other hand, students who live at home with their families probably have household responsibilities while students who rent a room with another family are not usually expected to do housework. In addition, students who value independence will probably prefer not to live with their parents.

Despite these differences there are important similarities between the two situations. Students who live in a family situation don't often feel lonely. There are usually people around for them to interact with. Also, in a family situation, students have the convenience of home-cooked meals; they don't have to spend time shopping for and cooking food, and the food is probably better than fast food or food from the school cafeteria. Finally, if they get sick or some other emergency happens, the family can help them. Because of these important aspects, both of these situations are less stressful than other, more independent living arrangements.

Focus on Testing

Listing Ideas for a Comparison

In Activity 1, you practiced listing similarities and differences between living situations. It's particularly useful to list ideas like these when you have to write a comparison for a timed writing test. Before you start writing, jot down everything that comes to mind on the topic. You'll quickly see that you have a lot to say, maybe even too much. Group the similarities and the differences, and cross out anything that is unrelated or unimportant. Then use what you have left to write your essay.

Timed Activity: 5 Minutes

Choose one topic from the following list. Brainstorm as many similarities and differences as you can. Then put them into two groups. When you are finished, compare your list with the list of another student who chose the same topic.

Topics
Compare two cities
Compare two sports
Compare cats and dogs

Writing Topic Sentences

11 Look at the first sentence of the composition on page 115. It is the topic sentence of the whole composition and identifies the situations that the writer is comparing. Which part focuses on the similarities? Which part focuses on the differences?

12 Tell whether the focus of the compositions with these topic sentences is on similarities or differences.

1. One of the most drastic changes that students going away to college face is the change from living at home with their families to living in a dorm with hundreds of other students.
2. If you don't mind sharing a room in a dormitory, then you will probably enjoy apartment living because there are many important similarities.

13 Write a topic sentence for your paragraph. You can use structures similar to the ones in Activity 12.

Analyzing the Organization of a Composition

14 Answer these questions about the organization of the composition "Family Living" on pages 115–116.

1. Which paragraph describes the similarities? Which one describes the differences? What is the topic sentence of the second paragraph?
2. Look at these words and expressions. Which ones does the writer use to show similarities? Which ones show differences?

   both while on the other hand more less
3. What transitional expressions does the writer use when mentioning additional similarities and differences?
4. Does the writer use any comparative structures (*more/less* + adjective, adjective + *-er*)?

PART 2 Write

Developing Cohesion and Style

Using Comparatives and Superlatives

Comparatives

To compare two people or things, use the pattern adjective + *-er* (+ *than*) or *more/less* + adjective (+ *than*).

Examples	Notes
A rooming house is *cheaper than* a dorm. (A rooming house is *cheaper*.)	One-syllable adjectives usually take the *-er* (+ *than*) ending.
Dorms are *noisier than* apartments. (Dorms are *noisier.*)	Two-syllable adjectives can take either the *-er* (+ *than*) ending or the words *more* or *less* (+ *than*).
An apartment is *more expensive than* a dorm. (An apartment is more *expensive.*)	Adjectives with more than two syllables always take *more* or *less* (+ *than*).
Paul is *happier than* Jack is about living in a dorm.	With two-syllable adjectives that end in *-y*, change the *y* to *i* before adding *-er.*
Apartments are *better than* dorms. Living in a dorm is *worse than* living at home.	Some irregular comparatives include *good-better; bad-worse; far-farther/further*

Superlatives

To describe something that has the greatest or least amount of a quality compared to two or more other things, use the pattern *the* + adjective + *-est* or *the* + *most/least* + adjective.

Examples	**Notes**
Living at home is *the cheapest* accommodation you can find.	One-syllable adjectives usually take the *-est* ending. Most adjectives with more than one syllable take *most/least.*
For many students, apartment life is probably *the most difficult.*	
A dorm offers *the least privacy.*	
Living in an apartment is *the best situation* for independent people.	Irregular superlatives include *the best; the worst; the farthest/furthest.*
Living at home is *the worst choice* if you want to be independent.	

1 Write the sentences using the comparative or superlative forms of the adjectives in parentheses.

1. A rooming house is ___more economical___ (economical) than an apartment.
2. Of all the possibilities, students probably feel ____________________ (free) in an apartment.
3. Even though there are campus police, it's hard to say that living on campus is ____________________ (safe) than living off.
4. My room is small but it's ____________________ (cozy) than my room in the dorm.
5. For many people, dorm life is the ____________________ (stressful).
6. Sharing an apartment with a few other students can be ____________________ (cheap) than living in a dorm.
7. Staying in a dormitory on campus is usually the ____________________ (convenient) living situation because you are close to classes.
8. I have lived in a dorm, an apartment, and at home. I thought that the dorm was the ____________________ (good).

9. Many parents think that living in a dorm is ____________________ (safe) than living in an apartment.

10. Dormitory food is often ____________________ (bad) than food you can cook yourself, even if you are not a great cook.

Using Both *in Comparisons*

There are several different ways to use *both* in a sentence that shows similarities.

1. Before nouns:

   Example
   Both situations are safe and inexpensive.

2. As a pronoun:

   Example
   Both are safe and inexpensive.

3. With verbs (note the position of *both* with different types of verbs):

   Examples
   They are *both* safe and inexpensive. (*Both* follows the verb *be.*)
   They have *both* given me a lot. (*Both* follows the first auxiliary verb.)
   They *both* offer convenience. (*Both* goes before one-word verbs except *be.*)

Using Neither *in Comparisons*

You can use *neither* to show negative similarities. Note that *neither* is always singular.

1. With *nor:*

   Example
   Neither living in a dorm *nor* sharing an apartment is ideal.

2. Before a singular noun:

   Example
   Neither situation is ideal.

3. As a pronoun:

   Example
   Neither is ideal.

2 Write sentences about the rules and facilities at the rooming house and the dormitory using *both* or *neither*. The first one is done as an example. (Note: a rooming house is a house where several students rent rooms. The landlord or landlady lives in the home too. Students do their own cooking.)

1. allow / smoking

   Neither the dormitory *nor* the rooming house allows smoking.
   ___

2. have / kitchen

   ___

3. play / loud music

   ___

4. television / available

   ___

5. allow / male visitors

   ___

6. require permission / overnight guests

   ___

3 Write two sentences about the similarities of the situations you chose. Use *neither* or *both.*

___

___

Using While *to Show Contrast*

You can use *while* to show two different or opposite ideas in a sentence. Note that you can use *while* before either clause of the sentence and that a comma is used in both sentences.

Examples

While living at home is inexpensive, sharing an apartment can cost a lot of money.

Living at home is inexpensive, *while* sharing an apartment can cost a lot of money

4 Look at these lists showing the differences between living in a dormitory and living in an apartment or with a family. Write two sentences with *while* to show the differences as in the preceding examples.

Living in a Dormitory	Living in an Apartment or with a Family
■ is less expensive	■ may require a long commute
■ don't have household chores	■ you feel part of the community
■ must share a room	■ it's possible to have a room to yourself
■ you are never lonely	■ you may feel separated from campus life
■ must eat cafeteria food	■ you can cook your own food or go to restaurants

Using Expressions of Contrast: In Contrast *and* On the Other Hand

The expressions *in contrast* and *on the other hand* have similar meanings. You can use them to present information that is different from or the opposite of some previous information.

Examples	**Notes**
Renting an apartment can be expensive. *In contrast,* living at home is inexpensive.	*In contrast* is used to contrast two different or opposite things.
Living at home is inexpensive. Renting an apartment, *in contrast,* is more expensive.	For variety, you can use *in contrast* after the subject; if you do, use two commas.
An apartment gives you more privacy. *On the other hand,* dorm life is a lot of fun. Renting a room is more expensive. *On the other hand,* you have little household responsibility.	*On the other hand* is often used to contrast advantages and disadvantages of the same thing (for example, renting a room).

5 In the following sentences, insert *in addition* to show additional similar information. Insert *in contrast* or *on the other hand* to show contrasting information.

1. Living in a dorm means that you are always surrounded by people. Apartment life can be quite lonely.

   Living in a dorm means that you are always surrounded by people. In contrast, apartment life can be quite lonely.

2. A rooming house is a good solution for those who like small groups of people. It's cheaper than living in a dormitory.

   ____

3. In an apartment, you can usually cook your own meals. In a dorm you usually have to eat cafeteria food or go to restaurants.

   ____

4. Living in a dorm is an exciting new experience. Staying at home with your family is just like being in high school.

   ____

5. Living with another family can be awkward. It's more expensive than staying with your family.

   ____

6 Complete the following sentences.

1. Having your own apartment can be a lot of work. In contrast, ______________________________

2. Apartments are often expensive. On the other hand, ______________________________

3. Rooming houses usually only have a few students. In contrast, ______________________________

4. Cooking your own food can be an advantage. On the other hand, ________

____

5. Students who live in apartments have a lot of responsibilities. In contrast,

____

____

Writing the First Draft

7 Write your composition using the organization you came up with at the beginning of this chapter. Use *both* and *neither* to show similarities. Use *while, in contrast, on the other hand* to show differences. You can also use *however* and *although* to show contrast. Write on every other line so that you can revise your paragraph.

PART 3 Edit and Revise

Editing Practice

1 Edit this paragraph for errors in the use of comparatives and superlatives.

The decision about whether to live on or off campus is a very important one. It may affect your whole college career. Both situations have advantages and disadvantages and which one you choose depends a lot on what is important to you. For example, on-campus housing is generally much convenienter than off-campus housing. It's more easy to get to class, especially early in the morning. Students who live on campus are also more closer to facilities such as the library and gym. On the other hand, in a dorm, you usually have to share a room, while off-campus housing can be much more private and least noisy. Cafeteria food is another disadvantage of on-campus housing. Students on special diets will often find it difficult to live in a dormitory than to live in a rooming house or apartment, where they can cook for themselves.

Editing Your Writing

2 Edit your composition, using the following checklist. First, check your paragraph for content, organization, cohesion, and style, using items 1, 2, and 3 in the checklist. Then edit your paragraph for grammar and form, using items 4 and 5.

Editing Checklist

1. Content

   Does your composition list all the similarities and differences you think are important?

2. Organization
   a. Does the topic sentence mention both similarities and differences even though it focuses on one or the other?
   b. Does one paragraph deal with differences and the other with similarities?

3. Cohesion and Style

   Have you used such expressions as *both, neither, in contrast, on the other hand,* and *while*?

4. Grammar
   a. Have you used gerunds correctly?
   b. Have you used comparatives and superlatives correctly?

5. Form
   a. Have you used a capital letter to begin each sentence?
   b. Have you used a period to end each sentence?

Peer Editing

3 Exchange papers with another student and edit each other's compositions. Discuss any questions you have with your partner.

Writing the Second Draft

4 Rewrite your composition neatly, using correct form. Then give it to your teacher for comments.

PART 4

A Step Beyond

Expansion Activities

1 Find a comparison for two things or two people in a newspaper or magazine. Note the words and expressions the writer uses in the comparison. Is he or she focusing mainly on differences or similarities?

2 Write a paragraph comparing two movies that you have seen. When you finish, give your paragraph to a partner to read.

Journal Writing

3 Write in your journal for fifteen minutes about one or both of the following topics.

1. Write about the similarities and differences between your high school and your college.
2. Write a comparison of two things or two people. You may choose types of music, cities, kinds of transportation, politicians, anything that has basis for comparison.

Video Activities: The Coffee Lover

Before You Watch. Discuss the following questions in a group.

1. Do you like to drink coffee? Why?
2. How would you feel if you drank ten cups of coffee every day?
3. As far as you know, does coffee cause health problems for some people?

Watch. Discuss the following questions with your classmates.

1. How many cups of coffee does Kat drink each day?
2. Does she plan to stop drinking coffee?

Watch Again. Read the statements below. Decide if they are true (T) or false (F). Then watch the video again to check your answers.

1. _____ Kat has worked in the same place for 45 years.
2. _____ Kat doesn't drink coffee in the evening.
3. _____ Scientists now believe that coffee raises cholesterol levels.
4. _____ If you drink too much coffee, it can make your hands shake.
5. _____ If your heart is weak, drinking coffee will make it stronger.

After You Watch. Interview a classmate using the questions below. Fill in your own answers too.

Questions	Classmate's Answer	Your Answer
a. What is your favorite drink: coffee, tea, or something else?		
b. How many times a day do you drink it?		
c. How do you drink it (with milk or sugar, hot or cold, etc.)?		
d. Do you think you will ever stop drinking it?		

Use the information in the chart to write a paragraph about you and your classmate's favorite drink(s). Begin with a general statement about your similarity or difference. For example, "Both Charlie and I love to drink tea." Then use expressions of comparison and contrast in your sentences (for example, *both/neither, while, in contrast, on the other hand*).

Chapter 9

New Frontiers

IN THIS CHAPTER

You are going to write a description of a planet.

PART 1

Before You Write

Exploring Ideas

Obtaining Information from Pictures, Diagrams, and Tables

Students often have to use pictures, charts, and tables to get accurate information that they need to write about certain subjects. This is especially true in the physical and social sciences. In this chapter, you will practice getting information from these sources.

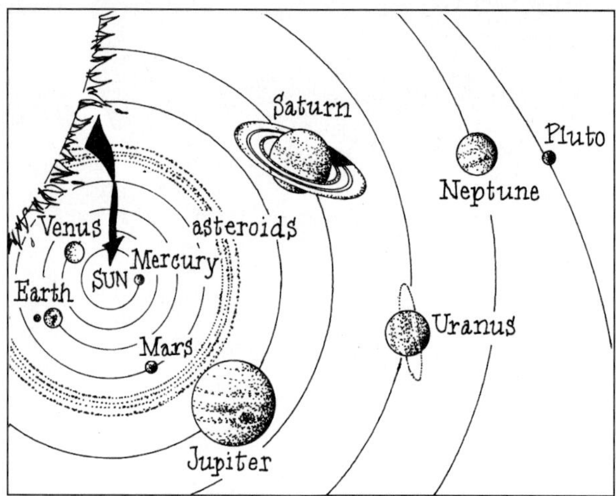

1 Look at the picture above and tables 1 and 2. Answer these questions.

1. Which planet is the largest?
2. Which planet has the most moons?
3. Which planet is the farthest from the sun?
4. Which planet rotates the most slowly?
5. Which planet has the fastest rotation?
6. How many moons does Neptune have?

Table 1

	Average Temperature	Diameter (in miles)	Number of Moons
Mercury	950°F on sunny side –350°F on dark side	3,032	0
Venus	800°F	7,523	0
Earth	59°F	7,928	1
Mars	extremes are 65°F to –190°F	4,218	2
Jupiter	19,300°F	88,900	16
Saturn	–228°F in atmosphere	74,900	23
Uranus	–270°F	31,800	15
Neptune	–330°F	30,800	8
Pluto	no information	1,400	1

Table 2

	Rotation	Distance from Sun (in millions of miles)	Revolution Around Sun
Mercury	58.6 days	36	88 days
Venus	243 days	67.2	224.7 days
Earth	23:56 hrs./mins.	92.9	365.26 days
Mars	24:37 hrs./mins.	141.5	687 days
Jupiter	9:55 hrs./mins.	483.4	11.9 years
Saturn	10:39 hrs./mins	884.6	29.5 years
Uranus	17 hrs.	1783.8	84 years
Neptune	17.7 hrs.	2793.9	164.79 years
Pluto	6.39 days	3890.5	247.7 years

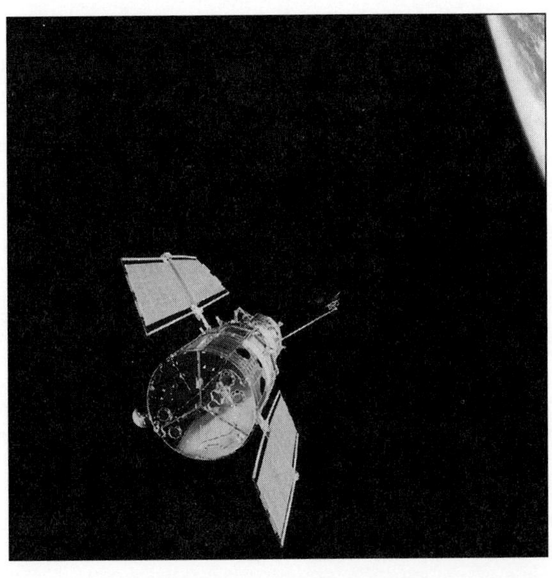

2 Look at tables 3 and 4. Answer the following questions.

1. When was Uranus discovered?
2. Which planets have been visited by spacecraft?
3. What is the atmosphere of Mars made of?
4. What is an interesting feature of Jupiter?
5. Who discovered Pluto?
6. Which planets have rings?

Table 3

	Composition of Atmosphere	Features
Mercury	little or none	craters like the moon
Venus	carbon dioxide	220-m.p.h winds
Earth	nitrogen, oxygen	
Mars	carbon dioxide, nitrogen, argon, oxygen	bright red color, some evidence of water, possible polar ice caps, volcanoes
Jupiter	hydrogen, helium, water, ammonia, methane	Great Red Spot, 25,000 miles long, several rings
Saturn	hydrogen, helium	huge system of rings of rock and ice
Uranus	hydrogen, helium, methane	10 rings and 15 moons
Neptune	hydrogen, helium, methane	cloudy, fluid atmosphere, and rocky core
Pluto	no information	consists of mainly water ice with a crust of methane ice

Table 4

	Planet Discovery	Exploration and New Discoveries
Mercury		In 1975 Mariner 210 found magnetic field that surprised scientists
Venus		Soviet spacecraft Venera 8 landed on Venus in 1972, sent information for one hour, was then destroyed by heat
Earth		
Mars		Viking spacecraft landed in 1975, analyzed soil samples
Jupiter		Pioneers 10 and 11 sent back photographs in 1975, Voyagers 1 and 2 sent back moving pictures in 1979
Saturn		Pioneer 10 sent back pictures in 1979
Uranus	Sir William Herschel 1781	Voyager 2 sent back pictures in 1986; discovered 10 new moons and strong magnetic field
Neptune	Gottfried Galle 1846	Voyager 2 flew by in 1989; discovered 3 rings and 6 new moons
Pluto	C. W. Tombaugh 1930	

3 In this chapter you are going to write a paragraph describing a planet. Select a planet other than Earth or Uranus. Study the information about the planet given on the preceding pages and complete this chart with the correct information. You may not be able to find information for every category for each planet.

Name: ____________________

Size: ____________________

Distance from the sun: ____________________

Composition: ____________________

Rotation: ____________________

Revolution around the sun: ____________________

Discovered: ____________________

Exploration / New discoveries: ____________________

____

Moons: ____________________

Interesting features: ____________________

____

What Do You Think?

Speculating

When you speculate about a subject, you make guesses based on what you already know about it. Speculating is useful when discussing or writing about scientific subjects.

Practice this skill by speculating about the planet you have chosen. First, answer these questions:

- Can the planet you have chosen to write about support life? Why or why not?
- What information from the chart helped you decide?

Now, share your answers with a partner.

Building Vocabulary

4 In answering the *What Do You Think?* questions, you may have found that you don't know the English words for some of the concepts you want to express. Find the words you need and add them to the following list.

Nouns	Verbs	Adjectives
atmosphere	be composed of	inhabited
composition	discover	uninhabited
diameter	explore	rocky
discoverer	inhabit	__________
discovery	revolve	__________
exploration	rotate	__________
orbit	orbit	__________
revolution	__________	__________
rotation	__________	__________
__________	__________	__________
__________	__________	__________
__________	__________	__________
__________	__________	__________

A view of earth from outer space

5 Look at the following groups of words and answer the questions.

composition	**be composed of**
exploration	**explore**
revolution	**revolve**
rotation	**rotate**

1. What is the function of the suffix *–tion?*
2. Can you think of any other verb/noun pairs that end in *–tion*?
3. What is the function of the suffix *–ed* in this case?

   inhabit **inhabited** **uninhabited**
4. What is the function of the prefix *un-* in number three?
5. Can you think of any other adjective pairs in which one word begins with *un-*?
6. What is the difference between these two nouns?

   discovery **discoverer**
7. Can you think of any other nouns that end in *–er*?

6 In writing about a planet, you will probably need to use expressions to describe the planet's position, movements, and composition. What other expressions can you think of? Add them to the list.

Location / Motion	**Composition**
is surrounded by	is composed of
lies between	is made up of (more than one item)
passes by/passes close to	is made of (only one item)
revolves around	________________
rotates	________________
________________	________________
________________	________________

Examples

The atmosphere of Saturn is composed of hydrogen and helium.

Two moons revolve around Mars.

Organizing Ideas

Making Comparisons

One way to make your paragraph more interesting is to tell the reader how the planet you are writing about is different from Earth or the other planets.

7 Look at your notes. Compare the planet you chose to Earth. Answer these questions.

1. Is it very much larger or smaller?
2. Does it have a much longer or shorter period of rotation / revolution?
3. Is it much hotter or colder?
4. Is it much farther from the sun?

8 Think of some other ways to compare Earth and the planet you chose.

____

____

____

____

9 Compare the planet you chose to the other planets. Answer these questions.

1. Is it the largest or one of the largest/the smallest or one of the smallest?
2. Is its atmosphere very different from the others?
3. Do scientists know a lot more or less about it than they do about other planets?

10 Finally, think of some other ways to compare your planet to the others in the solar system. Make notes of any interesting comparisons you have found. Remember, the greater the difference, the more interesting your comparison will be.

Focus on Testing

Making Comparisons Interesting

Activities 7 and 9 ask you to answer questions about the notes you made on your planet. Asking yourself questions like these will help you make your writing more interesting when you have to write a comparison for a timed test. Before you start writing in a testing situation, think of as many ways to compare your subjects as possible. Ask yourself questions that help you explore these areas. Jot down your answers and use them in your essay.

Timed Activity: 5 Minutes

Pretend that you are taking an essay test. In this essay, you have to compare your country to other countries. Write down as many types of comparisons as you can think of. Then connect them to make a cluster diagram. Give yourself five minutes to complete this task. Then compare your ideas with your classmates'.

Ordering Information in a Paragraph

In writing about your planet, you do not have to present information in any particular order. However, it is important to keep related information together.

11 These six topics describe the information given in the paragraph that follows. The topics are not in the correct order. Read the paragraph. Then number the topics according to the order in which they are presented in the paragraph. The first one is done for you.

_____ Exploration

_____ Discovery

_____ Length of year, day

_____ Composition of atmosphere

__1__ Position

_____ Features

Uranus, the seventh planet in the solar system, lies between the planets of Saturn and Neptune. Uranus's orbit is much larger than Earth's. It takes this planet 84 Earth-years to complete its trip around the sun. However, a day on Uranus is shorter than a day on Earth. It lasts only seventeen hours. Uranus was discovered in 1781 by the British astronomer Sir William Herschel. In 1986, the Voyager 2 spaceship passed by Uranus and took pictures. Before this exploration, not much was known about the planet. Scientific studies have now shown that its atmosphere is composed of hydrogen, helium, and methane and has a temperature of approximately –270°F. The planet has deep oceans of very hot water and a bright glow. The Voyager 2 pictures also showed that Uranus has ten rings and fifteen moons. Scientists hope to learn much more about this distant planet in the future.

---

12 Look at the notes for your paragraph and put them in the order you wish to state them.

____

____

____

____

PART 2

Write

Developing Cohesion and Style

Using the Passive Voice

The passive voice is used in both spoken and written English. It is often used in scientific or technical writing. In sentences in the active voice, the main focus is on the subject (the agent or doer of the action). In the passive voice, the main focus is on the object (the person or thing acted upon). Compare the following:

Active Voice: Nine planets *orbit* the sun. (subject: Nine planets; object: the sun) — *Main Focus* = nine planets

Passive Voice: The sun *is orbited by* nine planets. (subject: The sun; agent: nine planets) — *Main Focus* = the sun

All passive voice sentences contain a form of *be* + the past participle of the main verb. *By* + agent noun can be used in a passive voice sentence to tell who or what performed the action of a verb. *By* + agent is used in a passive sentence with new or important information; if the information is not important, it can be omitted.

Examples	Notes
Active Sir William Herschel *discovered* Uranus. **Passive** Uranus *was discovered by* Sir William Herschel.	The subject *Sir William Herschel* is important; it cannot be omitted from this passive sentence.
Active People *make* telescopes with a series of lenses. **Passive** Telescopes *are made* by people with a series of lenses.	The subject *people* is obvious. It is not important to the sentence. It can be omitted from the passive sentence.

Note: The following verbs are often used in the passive voice, but they usually do not use *by*. Instead, other prepositions follow these verbs.

The moon is not *composed of* green cheese.
made (up) of

Satellites *are used to* explore space.
used for exploring space

She is *known for* her scientific discoveries.
noted for

1 Complete the following paragraph with the appropriate passive or active forms of the verbs in parentheses. Don't forget to put the verb in the correct tense.

The Moon

A view of the moon

The moon ___orbits___ [1] (orbit) the Earth the way the Earth ____________ [2] (orbit) the sun. Scientists believe that the moon ____________ [3] (form) at about the same time as the Earth. They now know that it ____________ [4] (make up of) many of the same materials. But scientists ____________ [5] (find) that the moon is different from the Earth in many ways. For example, the moon ____________ [6] (have) no atmosphere to carry sound; as a result, no matter what ____________ [7] (happen) on the moon's surface, no sound ____________ [8] (hear). Without an atmosphere, water ____________ [9] (disappear) into space. That is why no water can ____________ [10] (find) on the surface of the moon, although some water ____________ [11] (trap) inside rocks. Without water, there can ____________ [12] (be) no weather. So if you go to the moon, you will never ____________ [13] (see) a cloud, ____________ [14] (get) wet in a rainstorm, or ____________ [15] (feel) the wind blow.

2 Look at the notes you made for your paragraph. Write three sentences in the passive voice about your planet based on your notes. Show your sentences to a classmate. Can he or she find any errors?

Varying Word Order: With + Noun Phrase

You can make your paragraph more interesting by changing the order of the elements in your sentence. For example, you can occasionally begin a sentence with a clause using *with* + noun phrase.

When you use this type of clause, you must make sure that the noun modifed by the clause comes directly after the clause. Compare the following:

Incorrect: *With a temperature of 800°F,* no life could survive on Venus.

Correct: *With a temperature of 800°F,* Venus is much too hot for life to survive.

The second sentence is correct because *Venus* (not *no life*) has a temperature of 800°F.

3 Match the clauses in Column A with the clauses in Column B. Use the tables on pages 129–130 if necessary.

	A		B
1.	d With its beautiful rings,	a.	Mars has interested astronomers for a long time.
2.	_____ With a diameter of only 1,400 miles,	b.	Venus cannot support life.
3.	_____ With a daytime temperature of 800°F,	c.	Earth looks like a blue ball from space.
4.	_____ With its bright red color and changing surface features,	d.	Saturn is the most spectacular planet in the solar system.
5.	_____ With its large oceans,	e.	Pluto is the smallest planet in the solar system.

4 Write a sentence about your planet using *with* + noun phrase.

____

____

Using Unlike + *Noun Phrase to Show Contrast*

Another way to make your paragraph more interesting is to begin a sentence by contrasting the planet you are writing about to Earth or to the other planets.

Examples

Unlike all the other planets, Venus rotates from west to east.

Unlike Earth, Mercury has no atmosphere.

5 Complete each of the following sentences.

1. Unlike Earth, Mars ____

____

2. Unlike Uranus and Neptune, Pluto ____

____

3. Unlike Earth, Jupiter ____

____

4. Unlike the other planets, Mercury ____

____

Giving Reasons with Because of *+ Noun Phrase and* Because *+ Clause*

You have already learned how to use *because* to connect two clauses.

Example

No one can live on Mercury *because* it is very hot.

The phrase *because of* is used with a noun phrase rather than a clause.

Example

No one can live on Mercury *because of* its high temperature.

Note that *because* is followed by a subject and a verb, but *because of* is followed by a noun. Both *because* and *because of* can be used in the middle or at the beginning of a sentence. When you begin a sentence with *because* or *because of,* you must remember to put a comma after the first clause or phrase.

Examples

Pluto is sometimes the eighth planet in the solar system *because* it has an irregular orbit.

Because it has an irregular orbit, Pluto is sometimes the eighth planet in the solar system.

Pluto is sometimes the eighth planet in the solar system *because of* its irregular orbit.

Because of its irregular orbit, Pluto is sometimes the eighth planet in the solar system.

6 Add *because of* or *because* to the phrases and clauses in Column A. Then match the terms in Column A and Column B to make logical sentences.

A

1. Because of its irregular orbit, d
2. ____________ its distance from the sun, _____
3. ____________ a desire to learn more about the solar system, _____
4. ____________ our need for oxygen, _____
5. ____________ it is close to Earth, _____
6. ____________ its orbit is much larger than Earth's, _____
7. ____________ pictures taken by Voyager 2, _____

B

a. Uranus takes 84 Earth-years to travel around the sun.
b. scientists learned that Uranus has ten rings and fifteen moons.
c. Pluto is extremely cold.
d. Pluto is sometimes the eighth planet in the solar system.
e. many spaceships have been launched.
f. Mars has always interested skywatchers.
g. human beings could not live on Mars.

7 Write a sentence about your planet using *because*. Then write another sentence about your planet using *because of*.

____

____

____

____

Writing the First Draft

8 Write your paragraph using the information from Activity 3 on page 131. Use the passive voice when necessary. Try to compare your planet with Earth or the other planets. Make your paragraph more interesting by varying the sentence structure with *unlike* + noun phrase and *with* + noun phrase. Give reasons with *because* or *because of*. Write on every other line so you can revise your paragraph easily.

PART 3 Edit and Revise

Editing Practice

1 Edit this paragraph for errors in the use of the passive voice, and rewrite it correctly.

Uranus

Uranus, the seventh planet in the solar system, locates between the planets of Saturn and Neptune. Uranus's orbit is much larger than Earth's. This planet's trip around the sun is taked in 84 Earth-years. However, a day on Uranus is shorter than a day on Earth. It lasts only seventeen hours. Uranus be discovered in 1781 by the British astronomer Sir William Herschel. In 1986 the Voyager 2 spaceship was passed by Uranus and took pictures; before that, not much had learned about its composition. Scientific studies have now been shown that its

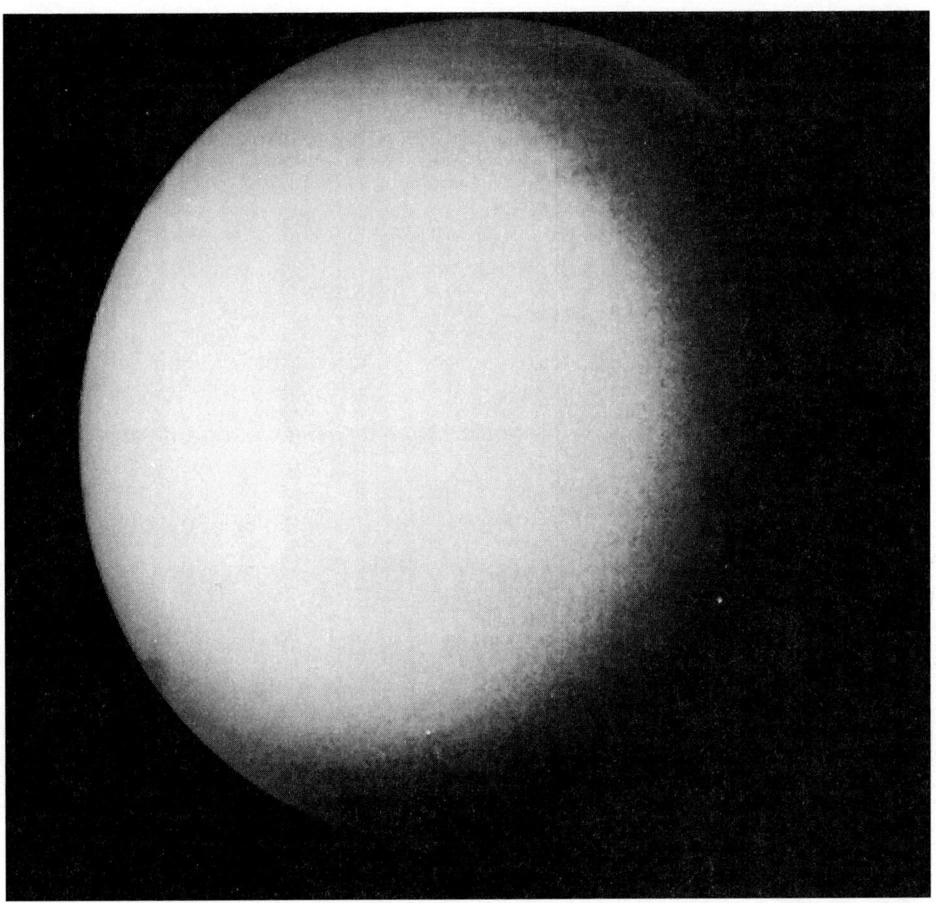

atmosphere is composing of hydrogen, helium, and methane and has a temperature of approximately 270°F. It has deep oceans of very hot water and a bright glow. The Voyager 2 pictures also show that Uranus has ten rings and fifteen moons. Scientists hope to learn much more about this distant planet in the future.

Editing Your Writing

2 Edit your composition using the following checklist. First, check your paragraph for content, organization, cohesion, and style, using items 1, 2, and 3 in the checklist. Then edit your paragraph for grammar and form, using items 4 and 5.

Editing Checklist

1. Content
   a. Is your information accurate?
   b. Have you made interesting comparisons?
2. Organization
   Is the information organized logically?
3. Cohesion and Style
   a. Did you vary the word order in some sentences, using *with* + noun phrase, *because* and *because of*?
   b. Did you use *unlike* + noun phrase to show contrast?
4. Grammar
   a. Did you use the passive voice correctly?
   b. Did you use correct tenses?
5. Form
   a. Did you use correct paragraph format? (indentation, division of words between syllables, margins)
   b. Did you use correct punctuation? (capitalization, commas, periods)
   c. Did you check the spelling of the words you are not sure of?

Peer Editing

3 Exchange papers with a classmate and edit each other's paragraphs. Circle or underline in pencil any words, phrases, or sentences that you don't understand or that you think need to be corrected. Then return your paragraphs. Discuss any questions you have with your partner.

Writing the Second Draft

4 After you edit your paragraph, rewrite it neatly, using correct form. Then give your composition to your teacher for comments.

PART 4

One Step Beyond

Expansion Activities

1 Find a description of how an object (for example, a tool or an appliance) is used. Directions or user's manuals (written material that comes with the product when you buy it) are good sources of this kind of writing. Note the use of the passive voice. Is it used a lot? A little? Are the instructions generally clear? Why or why not?

2 Imagine that your classmate is from another planet and has never seen an object that you use every day—for example, a telephone or a pencil. Write a paragraph describing it to him or her. Then exchange paragraphs.

3 In small groups, talk about some new discoveries and inventions you think will be made in the next twenty years. These might be discoveries or inventions in technology (e.g., new machines), medicine (e.g., new types of surgery or cures for diseases), astronomy (e.g., new information about planets), and so on. Make a list of your discoveries and inventions. In which countries do you think each of them will be made? Write the names of the countries next to the items on your list. When you finish your list, choose one discovery or invention that you believe will be most important. Put a check (✔) next to it.

Join another group of students and compare your lists. How are they similar? How are they different? Is there agreement about where you think the discoveries or inventions will be made? About which discovery or invention will be most important? What are some reasons for your choices?

Journal Writing

4 Write for fifteen minutes about one or more of the following topics.

1. Do you think that governments should be spending a lot of money on space exploration? Why or why not?
2. Think of an invention that you believe would make people's lives better. How would it be used? How would it improve people's lives?

Video Activities: Mapping the Human Genome

Before You Watch.

1. What determines each person's inherited characteristics—for example, eye color, height, or blood type?
2. Define the following terms: *gene, DNA.*
3. Tell what you know about research that is being done on the human genetic code.

Watch. Discuss the following questions with your classmates.

1. According to the video, what is the "book of life"?
2. What are the scientists in the video working on? What is their goal?

Watch Again. What are the benefits and disadvantages of mapping the human genetic code? Complete the chart.

Mapping the Genetic Code	
Benefits	**Disadvantages**

After You Watch. Write an answer to one of the questions below.

1. Which is greater, in your opinion: the benefits or the disadvantages of mapping the genetic code?
2. Can you think of additional advantages and disadvantages, besides the ones mentioned in the video?
3. Do you believe this kind of research should continue? Who should pay for it?

Chapter 10

Medicine, Myths, and Magic

IN THIS CHAPTER

You are going to write a composition taking a stand for or against the following statement.

> Astrology and fortune telling should be against the law because both cheat people.

PART 1

Before You Write

Exploring Ideas

Discussing Beliefs

1 Look at the pictures and discuss these questions.

1. What is happening in each picture?
2. Why do people go to fortune tellers?
3. What are some ways of predicting the future?

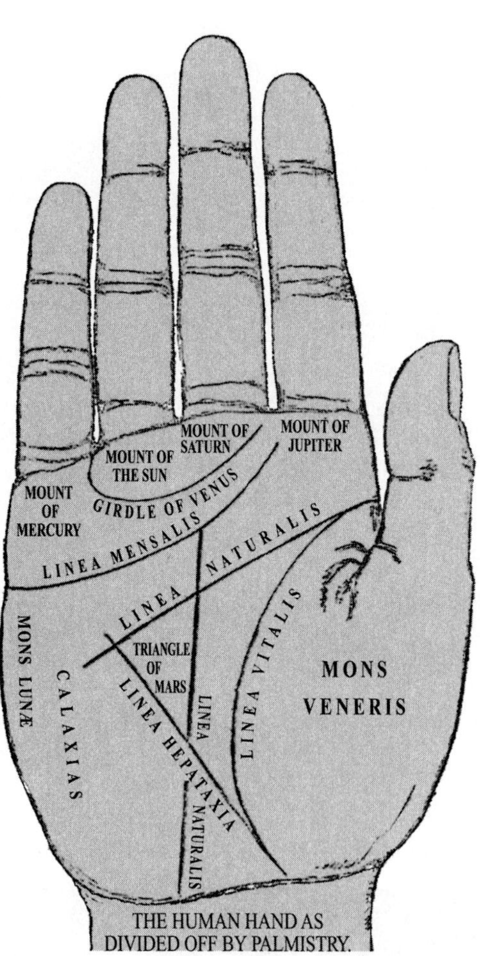

Building Vocabulary

2 Look at the following list of words. Add vocabulary from your discussion.

Nouns	Verbs	Adjectives	Other
crystal ball	predict	superstitious	____________
tea leaves	cheat	gullible	____________
palm-reading	lie	naïve	____________
belief	consult	____________	____________
spirit	prove	____________	____________
faith healer	____________	____________	____________
tarot cards	____________	____________	____________
coffee grounds	____________	____________	____________
fortune teller	____________	____________	____________

3 Work in small groups to complete the following chart. Use a dictionary to help you.

Nouns	Verbs	Adjectives
healer		------------
faith	------------	
	consult	------------
	------------	superstitious
spirit	------------	
	prediction	
belief		
	lie	------------
	prove	

What Do You Think?

Making a Persuasive Argument

The subject that you are going to write about concerns your personal beliefs. However, saying that you agree with fortune telling because you have faith in fortune tellers is not a strong persuasive argument. You have to support your opinion by telling people why you think that fortune telling is good or bad.

Practice this skill by studying the following statements from a composition about faith healing. (Note: Faith healers are people who claim to cure people with prayer rather than medicines and other treatments.) Decide if each statement offers a persuasive argument in support of the following statement.

Faith healers are valuable members of society.

_____ I believe in faith healing.
_____ My neighbor is a faith healer and she is very nice.
_____ They offer hope when medical science cannot.
_____ They cure some people.
_____ My aunt was cured by a faith healer.
_____ Doctors don't like faith healers.
_____ Faith healers are good people.

---

4 Do you agree or disagree with this statement?

> Astrology and fortune telling should be against the law because both cheat people.

Think of at least three reasons that support your opinion. Write them here.

____

____

____

Organizing Ideas

Focusing on a Topic

You are going to write a three-point argumentative composition. In this essay, you will give three reasons to support your opinion. This composition will be at least five paragraphs long. It should be organized like this:

Paragraph 1: Introduction: State your opinion on the topic.
Paragraph 2: Develop the first reason for your opinion with a detailed example.
Paragraph 3: Develop the second reason for your opinion with a detailed example.
Paragraph 4: Develop the third reason for your opinion with a detailed example.
Paragraph 5: Conclusion: Write a summary of your point of view.

In this kind of writing, it is important to choose a specific topic and focus on it clearly.

5 Read these introductions to an argumentative composition on the topic "Faith healers are valuable members of society because they offer hope when modern medicine cannot." How is the focus of each composition different? Discuss your answers in small groups.

1. Faith healers are simply thieves who take advantage of sick people by offering them the promise of a cure even when they know that all hope is lost.
2. Modern science does not have all the answers, especially when it comes to spiritual matters. Doctors are often wrong and "miracle cures" do happen.
3. It is amazing that in today's world there are still people who rely on superstition rather than science. Our schools are obviously not doing enough to educate people in scientific thinking.
4. When people spend thousands of dollars on medical cures that are not successful, no one says that the doctors were trying to cheat their patients. However, when a faith healer is not successful, everyone assumes the worst.

6 Write the introduction for your composition about fortune telling and astrology. State your opinion clearly and focus it on one particular idea.

___

___

___

___

___

Focus on Testing

Writing a Five-Paragraph Essay Exam

When you write an essay that has more than one paragraph, you must be careful how you divide the information. The first paragraph is usually an introduction and the last paragraph is usually a conclusion. These paragraphs can be just two or three sentences. They often say similar things. The three inner paragraphs, however, should each deal with a different point. Before you begin to write think about what you are going to say in each paragraph. Write an outline that is divided into five parts.

Timed Activity: 10 Minutes

Write an outline for a five-paragraph essay on one of the following topics.

1. Western Medicine Doesn't Have All the Answers
2. Homemade Cures that Work

Compare your outline with a partner's. Does each paragraph focus on a different point?

Supporting an Argument with Examples

Good writers support their opinions with examples. You can use examples from your own experience or cases you have read or heard about.

7 What example is given in this composition? Underline it.

Misplaced Faith

Faith healers may not all be liars and cheaters but I think that even those who want to help are dangerous. Modern medicine does not have all the answers for every disease. However, doctors today can keep people alive a lot longer, even if they cannot always cure them. Going to a faith healer is a risky thing to do, even if science cannot solve your problem.

People who go to faith healers may think that they are getting help when they are not. Even worse, the practices of some faith healers may actually harm their patients.

I once knew a woman who had cancer. When the doctors told her that she needed an operation, she decided to go to a faith healer. This man promised her that he would cure her cancer in three months. He gave her a special soap to use. He said that the soap was very expensive, so he charged her a lot of money. Three months later, she was much sicker and much poorer. She went back to the doctors but it was too late. She died two months later.

There are many stories like this one. People who are very sick are often frightened and confused. If they have never been to a hospital, they may not trust modern medicine. For many people, it is easier to trust a sympathetic person than modern technology.

Although I am sympathetic to the problems of people who are very ill, I do not agree that they should be able to go to faith healers. Through education we can teach people that modern science is our only hope for curing dangerous diseases.

---

8 Think of examples you can use to support your argument for or against fortune tellers. You can use examples from your own experience or from another story that you know. Write your examples on the following lines.

____

____

____

____

____

PART 2 Write

Developing Cohesion and Style

Using Transitions and Giving Examples

The example from the composition "Misplaced Faith" was introduced with this sentence:

I once knew a woman who had cancer.

That sentence is a transition sentence. It shows the purpose of the example. When you give an example, you can introduce it with expressions such as these:

____________ is a story/program/person that illustrates ____________.

An example of ____________ is ____________.

____________ is an example of ____________.

____________ shows ____________.

I once knew ____________.

1 Match these sentence parts to make transition sentences. Write the letter of the correct examples in the blanks after 1–4.

1. _____ My aunt's experience shows
2. _____ I once knew a man
3. _____ The care that my grandmother received from a faith healer
4. _____ My neighbor's story

a. who was cured by a faith healer.
b. showed me that modern medicine doesn't have all the answers.
c. that faith healing can work.
d. is an example of how faith healers can offer real hope to the sick.

2 Write a transition sentence to introduce the example you are going to use in your essay.

____

____

____

Using Quotations and Indirect Speech

Quotations can be used to support an argument in a composition. Both *direct quotations,* where you give the exact words of the speaker, and *indirect quotations,* where you give the general ideas of the speaker, can be used. (See Appendix 3 for the rules on punctuation of direct quotations.)

Examples Direct quotation: He said, "I don't want to take a lot of medicine."
Indirect quotation: He said (that) he didn't want to take a lot of medicine.

There are changes that you must make when you use indirect speech. Here are some of them.

Direct Speech		**Indirect Speech**
present tense *(eat/eats)*	changes to	past tense *(ate)*
present continuous *(am/is/are eating)*	changes to	past continuous *(was/were eating)*
past tense *(ate)*	changes to	past perfect *(had eaten)*
present perfect *(has/have eaten)*	changes to	past perfect *(had eaten)*
present perfect continuous *(has/have been eating)*	changes to	past perfect continuous *(had been eating)*
future *will (will eat)*	changes to	*would (would eat)*
I	changes to	he, she
you	changes to	he, she
we	changes to	they
me	changes to	him, her
us	changes to	them
today	changes to	that day
yesterday	changes to	the day before

3 Use the information in the preceding box to change these quotations to indirect speech.

1. She said, "I have never gone to a faith healer."

   She said she had never gone to a faith healer.

2. "We're going to cure you quickly," they promised.

3. "That faith healer stole all of my money," he said.

4. The woman said, "If you trust me, you will feel better."

5. The man said, "Yesterday I cured a woman of cancer. Today I am going to cure you."

4 Is there a direct or indirect quotation you can use in your composition? Write it here.

Making Generalizations

Generalizations made in English are different from those in many other languages. When English speakers make general statements with count nouns, they use the indefinite article *a/an* with singular count nouns. They do not use any article with plural count nouns or noncount nouns. They never use the definite article *the* in general statements.

Count Nouns

Examples

We should not stop people from going to faith healers.
plural

We should not stop a person from going to a faith healer.
singular

Noncount Nouns

Example

Modern *medicine* helps many people.

5 On a separate paper, write sentences using each of the nouns with a general meaning.

Example

technology

Medical technology saves many lives.

1. education
2. faith
3. hospital
4. machines
5. life
6. patients
7. medicine
8. doctor
9. parent
10. operations

Writing the First Draft

6 Write your composition. Use your introduction and example with its transition sentence. Use examples and quotations if you can. Write on every other line so you can revise your paragraph easily.

PART 3

Edit and Revise

Editing Practice

1 Edit these paragraphs and rewrite them correctly. Check the use of indefinite forms when marking generalizations. Then compare your edited paragraphs with the composition on pages 150–151.

Faith healers may not all be a liar and a cheater but I think that even those who want to help are dangerous. A modern medicine does not have all the answers for every disease. However, the doctor today can keep people alive a lot longer, even if they cannot always cure them. Going to a faith healer is a risky thing to do, even if the science cannot solve your problem.

People who go to the faith healer may think that they are getting help when they are not. Even worse, practices of some faith healers may actually harm their patients.

Editing Your Writing

2 Edit your composition, using the following checklist. First, check it for content, organization, cohesion, and style, using items 1, 2, and 3 in the checklist. Then edit your composition for grammar and form, using items 4 and 5.

Editing Checklist

1. Content
   a. Did you support your opinion with good reasons and information?
   b. Is your composition interesting?
2. Organization
   a. Do you have an introduction, supporting paragraphs, and a conclusion?
   b. Is your focus clear?
   c. Did you give examples to support your reasons?
3. Cohesion and Style
   a. Did you introduce your examples with transitions?
   b. Did you use quotations to support your argument?
4. Grammar
   a. Did you use indefinite forms correctly?
   b. Did you use *the* correctly in sentences with *of* + noun phrases?
5. Form
   a. Did you use correct essay form? (introduction, three supporting paragraphs, and a conclusion)
   b. Did you use correct paragraph format? (indentation, division of words between syllables, margins)
   c. Did you use correct punctuation? (capitalization, commas, periods)
   d. Did you check the spelling of the words you are not sure of?

Peer Editing

3 Exchange papers with a classmate and edit each other's compositions. Circle or underline in pencil any words, phrases, or sentences that you don't understand or that you think need to be corrected. Then return your compositions. Discuss any questions you have with your partner.

Writing the Second Draft

4 After you edit your composition, rewrite it neatly, using correct form. Then give your composition to your teacher for comments.

PART 4 A Step Beyond

Expansion Activities

1 Have a debate about the statement: "Astrology and fortune telling should be against the law because both cheat people." The class will divide into two teams, with one team taking the affirmative side and one the negative side.

First meet with the members of your team and read each others' compositions. Make a list of your arguments. Then try to guess what the other team will argue and think of reasons against their arguments (rebuttals).

Choose three students to represent each side. One will give the arguments (about five minutes), one the rebuttal (about three minutes), and one the summary (about three minutes).

2 Find a persuasive article in the editorial section of your local newspaper. With a partner, outline the article. Then answer these questions:

- How many paragraphs does it have?
- Is there an introductory paragraph?
- How many reasons for his or her opinion does the author present?
- What examples does the author use?
- Are you persuaded by his or her argument?
- Why or why not?

3 Write a three-paragraph essay taking the opposite side of the question you wrote about for this chapter. You may get opposite points of view by recalling what the other side said during the debate you held or by interviewing a classmate who disagrees with you.

Journal Writing

4 Write for fifteen minutes about one of the following topics.

1. Write about your opinion of faith healing.
2. Write in your journal on any topic you choose.

Video Activities: A New Treatment for Back Pain

Before You Watch.

1. In your culture, is there a difference between "scientific" and "alternative" types of medicines and treatments?
2. What are some ways you know to treat back pain?
3. The following words refer to the human nervous system. Review their meanings: *nerve, spinal cord, brain.* Share what you know about the way information from the body reaches the brain.

Watch. Read the following statements. Write (T) if they are true and (F) if they are false.

1. _____ The procedure uses electricity to reduce the patients' pain.
2. _____ The treatment takes place in a doctor's office.
3. _____ The treatments are painful.
4. _____ The pain relief from the procedure is immediate.

Watch Again. Take notes on the two patients before and during/after the needle treatment.

Patient	Before Treatment	During/After Treatment
Doris Dorry	-had back pain for 25 years -pain level was a "10"	
Judy Ellis		

After You Watch. Some people receive the best, most modern medical treatment in the world, yet they die of their illnesses. Other people have serious illnesses, yet they are able to recover with little or no help from medical doctors. Why do you think this is so? Do you know anyone who "miraculously" recovered from a serious illness? What was this person's "secret"? Write a paragraph about what you think.

Chapter 11

The Media

IN THIS CHAPTER

You are going to write a newspaper article.

PART 1

Before You Write

Exploring Ideas

Discussing a News Event

1 Look at the photos of a flood and an earthquake. Discuss what information you would expect to find in an article about each event.

2 Write five questions you would expect each article to answer.

The Flood

1. ____
2. ____
3. ____
4. ____
5. ____

The Earthquake

1. ____
2. ____
3. ____
4. ____
5. ____

3 In this chapter you are going to write a short article about a fire. Write five questions you would expect an article to answer about the fire in the photo.

1. ______________________________
____

2. ______________________________
____

3. ______________________________
____

4. ______________________________
____

5. ______________________________
____

What Do You Think?

Distinguishing Fact from Opinion

When a reporter writes an article about an event, he or she usually gives only facts. It is not appropriate for reporters to give their personal opinions or to include information that may or may not be correct.

Practice distinguishing fact from opinion. Read the following paragraph. Draw a line through any information that should not be included—information that is the reporter's opinion and not fact. When you finish, compare your results with a partner.

Fumes from Chemical Plant Send Dozens to Hospital

A cloud of sulfuric acid fumes sickened thirty-six people as it swept across downtown Middleport yesterday. The poisonous cloud came from the Kozar Chemical Plant in Santa Clara, California, which should be closed. Officials at the plant say that the sulfuric acid escaped as it was being transferred from one tank to another. I think this was very careless of the plant workers. Two weeks ago there was a similar accident at this plant. Most people believe that the plant officials should be fired for their carelessness.

Building Vocabulary

4 Add to this list any new vocabulary or expressions from your discussion and questions.

Nouns	Verbs	Adjectives	Other
blaze	break out	burned	overcome by smoke
fire company	injure	burning	
firefighters	rescue	heroic	
firetruck	save	hospitalized	
flames		dramatic	
inferno		courageous	
(the) injured			
smoke			
victim			

5 Complete the chart with the word forms. Use a dictionary to help you.

Verbs	Nouns	Adjectives
injure	______________	
rescue	______________	
	______________	courageous
	______________	hospitalized
	______________	heroic

Organizing Ideas

Answering Questions in an Article About an Event

The first paragraph of an article gives you the most important facts. It usually answers these questions, sometimes called the five Ws.

Who? What? Where? When? Why?

6 Read the following article. Then underline the words that answer the five W questions.

Missing Boaters Found off Cape Cod

A sixty-five-year-old man and his ten-year-old grandson were found yesterday by the Coast Guard after spending fifteen hours drifting in heavy seas. Joseph Miller, a retired teacher, and his grandson Eric Miller, both from Boston, said that the boat lost power just as they were about to return home about 4 P.M. on Thursday and that they were unable to get the engine started again. When the two did not return home by dark, Miller's daughter-in-law called the police. The small boat was found drifting about five miles off Cape Cod. The victims were all taken to Memorial Hospital where they are said to be in fair condition.

A Coast Guard search unit

7 Imagine that there has been a fire somewhere at your school. Take notes about this imaginary fire for your article. Answer these questions:

1. Who? ______________________________
2. What? ______________________________
3. Where? ______________________________
4. When? ______________________________
5. Why? ______________________________

Adding a Title

The titles of stories for newspapers and magazines must get the readers' attention in as few words as possible. Therefore the verb *be* and articles are often omitted.

Fact: A man was killed by a hit and run driver.
Title: Man Killed by Hit and Run Driver

Fact: A hurricane is approaching the East Coast.
Title: Hurricane Approaching East Coast

Fact: First National Bank was robbed by a man in a Santa Claus suit.
Title: First National Bank Robbed by Man in Santa Claus Suit

8 Rewrite these sentences as titles; omit any unnecessary words.

1. A provincial capital was taken over by guerrillas.
   Provincial Capital Taken Over
2. The Waldorf Art Museum was destroyed by an explosion.
   ____
3. Four people were killed in a plane crash.
   ____
4. Killer bees are threatening cattle in Texas.
   ____
5. A convicted murderer was executed.
   ____

9 Write a title for your article.

____

PART 2

Write

Developing Cohesion and Style

Using Relative Clauses (Review)

Read this paragraph.

> There was a fire in Middletown yesterday. It started in a warehouse and quickly spread to three nearby stores. The fire burned for four hours. The fire did $100,000 worth of damage. The fire killed one security guard and injured another.

The paragraph would sound much better if its five short sentences were combined into two longer sentences.

> A fire that started in a Middletown warehouse yesterday and quickly spread to three nearby stores did $100,000 worth of damage. The fire, which burned for four hours, killed one security guard and injured another.

Note that the combined sentences contain two different kinds of relative clauses. The relative clause in the first sentence does not have commas before and after it. This type of clause is called a restrictive relative clause. It contains information that is essential to the sentence and identifies the noun modified by answering the question "which one?"

The second type of relative clause is called a nonrestrictive relative clause. The information in a nonrestrictive relative clause is not essential to the sentence; it is set off by commas.

Using Restrictive Relative Clauses: Review

1 Combine the information in these sentences, using restrictive relative clauses.

1. A seventeen-year-old girl is in critical condition at Long Island Hospital. She was hit by a car last night.

   A seventeen-year-old girl who was hit by a car last night is in critical condition at Long Island Hospital
   ___

2. A volcano erupted on the island of Hawaii yesterday. It has destroyed ten homes.

   ___
   ___

3. Three children escaped without injury from their burning home. They were playing with matches.

____

____

4. The miners' strike will be settled this week. It has paralyzed Britain's coal industry.

____

____

5. A police officer wounded a robber. The robber was trying to steal an elderly woman's purse.

____

____

Using Nonrestrictive Relative Clauses

2 Combine the information in these sentences, using nonrestrictive relative clauses beginning with *who*, *which*, *whose*, *where*, or *when*. Remember to set off the clause with commas. (For information on punctuating relative clauses, see Appendix 3.)

1. Tracy O'Brian was crossing Morton Avenue at the time of the accident. She is a senior at Bayside High School.

   Tracy O'Brian, who is a senior at Bayside High School, was crossing Morton Avenue at the time of the accident.

2. The volcano has erupted several times in recent years. It is one of the most active volcanoes in the world.

____

____

3. The children were rescued by a neighbor. The children's mother was at the store.

____

____

4. Brian McDonald said that he believes the miners will go back to work next week. Brian McDonald is the head of the Miners' Union.

____

____

5. The elderly woman was rushed to Fairfield Hospital. The elderly woman had tried to fight off her attacker.

____

____

6. On Christmas Day two gunmen tried to rob a bank. On this day, most people are at home with their families.

____

____

7. In Thailand two tourists were arrested for sitting on the head of a statue of Buddha. In Thailand most people are Buddhists.

____

____

3 Rewrite this paragraph on a separate piece of paper. Combine the sentences within parentheses, using restrictive and nonrestrictive relative clauses.

(A tugboat disappeared off the Connecticut coast yesterday. The tugboat carried six crew members.) (The boat left Bridgeport harbor at 8:00 P.M. on Saturday. The tugboat was on its way out to sea.) (A helicopter was sent in search of the tugboat. The tugboat was supposed to arrive on Saturday night.) (The president of the tugboat company said that they will not stop searching until the tugboat is found. The president's son is aboard the tugboat.)

4 Look at the information you wrote for your paragraph. Write three sentences using restrictive and/or nonrestrictive relative clauses.

____

____

____

____

____

____

____

____

____

____

Writing the First Draft

5 Write your article using the questions you wrote in Activity 3 on page 161. Use relative clauses and be careful to omit unnecessary words. Write on every other line so you can revise your paragraph easily.

PART 3

Edit and Revise

Editing Practice

Using Commas with Nonrestrictive Clauses

1 Edit this article for the use of commas with nonrestrictive clauses.

Janet Reese a ten-year-old burn victim who was badly hurt in a kitchen fire two years ago wants to help other children. She is being treated at the Miami Burn Center and says that other children, who have gone through similar experiences, can get encouragement from her experience.

Specialists at the Burn Center a team of doctors and nurses who are among the best in the country are impressed by her courage and determination. The doctor, who is treating her, said that her courage and will to live were the things that really kept her alive. Janet is sending letters to other children, who have serious burns. She tells them that she was hurt, but she got better, and they can too.

Using Reduced Clauses

Good writers generally try to use as few words as possible. Therefore, they often leave out unnecessary words in relative clauses.
Here are two ways to do this:

1. You can omit the relative pronoun if it refers to the object of a restrictive relative clause.

   Example
   The man *that* the policeman caught was wearing a Santa Claus suit.
   The man the policeman caught was wearing a Santa Claus suit.

2. You can omit the relative pronoun and the auxiliary verb *be* in restrictive and nonrestrictive relative clauses.

   Examples
   First National Bank, *which is* protected by Benson Security, was robbed yesterday.
   First National Bank, protected by Benson Security, was robbed yesterday.
   The girl *who was* missing for two days was found unharmed.
   The girl missing for two days was found unharmed.
   Several firefighters *who were* on the scene were overcome by smoke.
   Several firefighters on the scene were overcome by smoke.

2 Read this paragraph and omit any unnecessary words.

Fire in Cameron Hotel

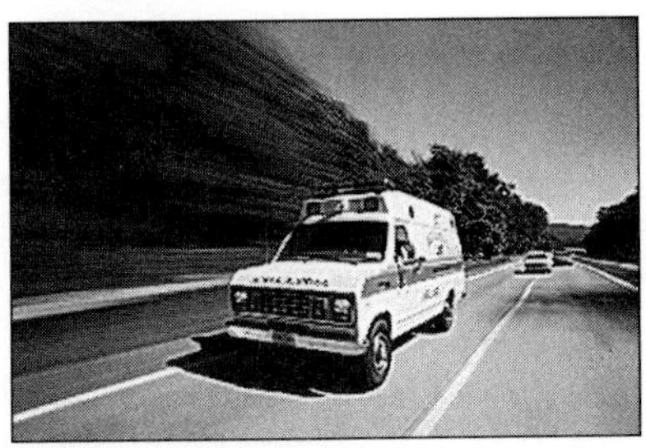

A two-alarm fire broke out on the sixth floor of the beautiful and expensive Cameron Hotel early yesterday. The fire, which was controlled by firefighters after four hours, caused extensive damage to the hotel, although no serious injuries were reported. The blaze started in a resident's room of the twelve-story hotel at 222 W. 23rd Street shortly after 3:00 A.M. Someone said that the blaze was caused by a guest who was smoking in bed. While they struggled to control the flames, four firefighters were overcome by smoke and taken to Roosevelt Hospital. Fire officials who were on the scene said that there will be an official investigation into the cause of the fire.

3 Look at the sentences you wrote for your article. Can you omit any words?

Focus on Testing

Checking for Mechanics

Good mechanics (punctuation and capitalization, spelling, and handwriting) make your writing easier to read. When you take a timed test, leave a few minutes at the end to check for mechanics. Look for one thing at a time (punctuation/capitalization, spelling, or handwriting). Also, try reading your essay backwards—that is, read the last sentence first, then the second-to-last, and so on. This makes mechanical mistakes easier to find.

Timed Activity: 2 Minutes

Find as many mechanical errors as you can in two minutes.

Local Man Won Lottery

James Kirk which is a mechanic at Willy's Auto Body, won the fifteen million dollar grand prize in the state lotterie last night. Mr. Kirk said that he had recieved the lottery ticket as a birthday gift from his brother Carl. We always buying lottery tickets on our birthdays. Two years ago I gave Carl a ticket and he won $200, said the surprised Mr. Kirk he also said that he planning to share the money with his brother but they don't decide how to divide it yet. For the moment he is still working but he expects to quit as soon as he gets the maney.

Editing Your Writing

4 Edit your article, using the following checklist. First, check your paragraph for content, organization, cohesion, and style, using items 1, 2, and 3 in the checklist. Then edit your paragraph for grammar and form, using items 4 and 5.

Editing Checklist

1. Content
   a. Is your article interesting?
   b. Does it provide enough detail?
2. Organization
   a. Does your article answer these questions: *Who? What? Where? When? Why?*
   b. Did you have an appropriate title?
   c. Did you include facts and not personal opinions?
3. Cohesion and Style
   a. Did you use restrictive relative clauses correctly?
   b. Did you use nonrestrictive relative clauses correctly?
4. Grammar
   a. Did you punctuate relative clauses correctly?
   b. Did you use correct verb tenses?
5. Form
   a. Did you use correct paragraph format? (indentation, division of words between syllables, margins)
   b. Did you use correct punctuation? (capitalization, commas, periods)
   c. Did you check the spelling of the words you are not sure of?

Peer Editing

5 Exchange papers with a classmate and edit each other's articles. Circle or underline in pencil any words, phrases, or sentences that you don't understand or that you think need to be corrected. Then return your articles. Discuss any questions you have with your partner.

Writing the Second Draft

6 After you edit your article, rewrite it neatly, using good form. Then give your article to your teacher for comments.

PART 4

A Step Beyond

Expansion Activities

1 Make a school newspaper. Choose some of the articles about the fire. Also write some other articles about anything interesting that has happened to the students at your school. You can write about accidents, important events, sports, family life, or achievements.

2 Find an article in a newspaper or a magazine on a subject that interests you. Try to find one that has three or more paragraphs. Read the article carefully. Then, without looking at it, summarize the information in the article in one sentence. (Hint: Answer as many of the *wh-* questions—"Who?" "What?" and so on—as you can in one well-written sentence.) Then expand your one-sentence summary to one paragraph. Exchange your work with a classmate. Give him or her the sentence to read first, then the paragraph, and, finally, the original article.

Journal Writing

3 Write for fifteen minutes about one of the following topics.

1. Write about the most frightening experience you have ever had.
2. Write about the saddest experience you have ever had.
3. Write about the happiest experience you have ever had.

Video Activities: Bye, Bye, Charlie Brown

Before You Watch. Discuss the following questions in a group.

1. Have you ever seen or read "Peanuts"? (In some countries it is called "Snoopy.") Tell what you know about this comic strip. Do you have a favorite character?
2. What other comic strips do you know?

Watch. Write answers to the following questions.

1. What did Charles Schultz think of the name "Peanuts"?

   ____

   ____

2. Why did Charles Schultz retire?

   ____

   ____

3. What unusual event happened on the day this video was made?

   ____

   ____

Watch Again. Fill in the missing details.

1. For nearly ____________ years, the comic strip Peanuts appeared in more than ____________ newspapers in ____________ different countries. It had approximately ____________ readers. It was first published in ____________.
2. Charles Schultz never liked the name "Peanuts" because it doesn't have ____________. He would have preferred to call the strip ____________.
3. The woman at the end of the video will miss the character called ____________.

After You Watch. Work in a group. Draw three or four boxes on a piece of paper, and write a simple comic strip. When all the groups are finished, compare the dialogues you wrote.

Chapter 12

With Liberty and Justice for All

IN THIS CHAPTER

You are going to write a proposal to solve a community problem.

PART 1

Before You Write

Exploring Ideas

Discussing Community Problems

1 Discuss the following photos. Each one shows a solution to a problem. What problem does each photo represent?

A new daycare center for the students and staff of a local community college

New low-cost housing for city residents

Volunteer tutor from home for the aged tutoring student from nearby school

2 List on the board some problems that people in your community or school have. Then choose a problem you are interested in and discuss possible solutions in small groups. Try to think of as many solutions as you can.

3 Choose a problem and write a proposal. Begin by proposing a solution to the problem. Use the word *should* to propose your solution. Then give one or two reasons that show who would benefit from your proposal. Use the words *would*, *might*, or *could* to give your reasons.

Example

> Our college should organize a program to help our community. For example, students who are planning to be teachers could volunteer to tutor young children. Those studying nursing or nutrition could start a health education program, and law students could help poor people understand their legal rights. This type of program would benefit the students as well as the community because it would give students practical experience.

Write your proposal on the lines.

____

____

____

____

What Do You Think?

Determining Realistic Solutions

It's easy to think of solutions to problems, but a good solution is one that is realistic. Consider a major city that has a serious air pollution problem, for example. Someone might propose closing downtown streets to car traffic as a means to cleaner air. But is this a realistic solution? What about people who must drive in order to earn their living? What about delivery trucks? What about businesses that service cars and trucks? Are people going to like this solution? Probably not. Asking questions like these about a solution to a problem can help you decide whether it is realistic.

Practice this skill with a partner by proposing solutions to the following problems. Then evaluate each other's solutions.

- Students are complaining about the food served in the school cafeteria.
- A teacher is not teaching what is in the syllabus.
- A foreign language class has forty-five students in it; the students feel they are not getting enough individual attention.
- Students are complaining about people skateboarding around campus during school hours.

---

4 Write two to four reasons why you think that your proposal is a good one.

1. ______________________________
2. ______________________________
3. ______________________________
4. ______________________________

Building Vocabulary

5 Add new vocabulary from your discussion to this list.

Nouns	Verbs	Adjectives	Other
advantage	propose	beneficial	
result	object (to)	costly	
disadvantage	organize	realistic	
establishment (of)	raise (objections)		
expense	improve		
	simplify		
	persuade		
	give _______ a chance		

6 Complete this chart with the correct form of the words. Use a dictionary to help you.

Nouns	Adjectives	Verbs
______________	costly	______________
______________		improve
______________		organize
______________	beneficial	benefit
establishment		______________
advantage	______________	
______________		propose
	simple	______________
problem	______________	
______________	expensive	
______________	______________	object
______________	______________	persuade

7 Look at the chart above and answer these questions.

1. What two suffixes change verbs to nouns?
2. What three suffixes change nouns to adjectives?

Organizing Ideas

Determining Who Your Audience Is

You are going to write a persuasive essay. In your essay, you will try to convince a group of people that your proposal is a good one. The arguments that you use will depend on who your audience is. For example, if you think that the classes in your school should be limited to twelve students, you will have to try to convince the school administration. If you think that students who speak a language other than English in the classroom should be fined, you will have to convince your classmates and your teacher.

8 Who is the audience for your essay?

____

____

Countering Objections to Your Proposal

Once you know who your audience is, try to think of some objections that they may have to your proposal. Imagine what their viewpoint is. For example, in answer to a proposal that classes in your school should be limited to twelve students, the school administrators might have these two objections:

1. There is no money to hire more teachers.
2. There are not enough classrooms to divide the classes.

To convince the administration that classes should be smaller, you will have to counter these objections. The best way to do this is to provide possible solutions to the objections.

9 In small groups, discuss some possible solutions to the administration's two objections. Write down your solutions. Then join another group of students. Compare your solutions. Are they similar or different? Which solutions are most realistic?

10 Look at this proposal:

> Students who speak their native language in the classroom should be fined twenty-five cents.

List two possible objections to this proposal.

1. ______
2. ______

List counter arguments to these objections.

1. ______
2. ______

11 Now list some objections that your audience might have to your proposal.

1. ______
2. ______
3. ______
4. ______

List possible counter arguments to these objections.

1. ______
2. ______
3. ______
4. ______

Making an Outline

Your composition will include an introductory paragraph and a closing paragraph. In addition, there will be one paragraph for each of your arguments and a paragraph listing possible objections and countering them. It is often easier to organize this type of writing by putting it in a simplified outline form:

I. Introductory paragraph: states proposal and lists arguments for it
II. Persuasive argument 1: develops the first argument and says why your proposal should be carried out
III. Persuasive argument 2: develops the second argument
IV. Counter arguments: counters objections
V. Concluding paragraph: summarizes reasons for the solution you proposed

Here is a sample outline.

I. Introductory paragraph
    1. ABC English Language Academy should start a cooperative day-care center.
    2. It would benefit both the community and the school.
II. Argument 1
    1. It would benefit the community:
        a. Mothers of young children cannot attend English classes because they cannot afford to hire babysitters.
        b. Many women have no chance to learn English and feel uncomfortable living in the United States.
        c. Their children do not learn English until they go to school.
        d. Mothers cannot help children with their schoolwork because of the language barrier.
III. Argument 2
    1. It would benefit the school:
        a. People would feel that the school was really interested in helping the community (public relations).
        b. It would help attract a better staff.
        c. It would increase efficiency because staff members would work harder if they weren't worried about their children.
        d. School enrollment would increase.
IV. Counter arguments
    1. To the objection that it would be difficult for the school to organize:
        a. A student-staff organizing committee could be created.
        b. Several interested students and staff members have experience working in day-care centers.
        c. The committee would take complete responsibility for obtaining licenses and other such tasks.
    2. To the objection that it would cost the school too much money:
        a. Because it would be a cooperative, students and staff would volunteer their time.
        b. Participating students and staff members could bring in used toys, books, and so on.
        c. A small enrollment fee could be used to cover the cost of furniture and other necessary items.
        d. There is a possibility that the government would help fund the center.
V. Concluding paragraph

Children at a day-care center

12 Now make a similar outline for your essay. Your essay may have from four to six paragraphs. Remember that each separate argument should be stated in a new paragraph.

Focus on Testing

Making an Outline

You should make an outline when you are taking a timed test. You will have less time in a testing situation, so you will have to make a less complete outline than you would at home. (For example, you can simply number the items in place rather than copying them over in outline form.) However, having at least the following will make your writing task a lot easier:

- A statement of the main idea of the entire essay—this will be in your introductory paragraph.
- A list of ideas to support your main idea—these will be the topic sentences of each of your body paragraphs.
- Two or more examples for each supporting idea—these will develop each of your body paragraphs.

Timed Activity: 7 Minutes

Choose one of the following topics and brainstorm ideas for writing an essay. Then choose the ideas you wish to include and arrange them in a simple outline form as given in the preceding box. Give yourself seven minutes to do this activity. Then compare your outline with another student who chose the same topic.

1. The university medical school should open a free clinic for the community.
2. All students in our school should have to do some community service activity before they graduate.

PART 2

Write

Developing Cohesion and Style

Using the Conditional Mood

Do these sentences refer to conditions that exist now or to conditions that might or could exist if something else were true?

1. If I were rich, I would buy a Mercedes Benz.
2. If you paid attention in class, you could learn to speak English.
3. If Ricardo tried jogging, he might lose weight.

In your essay, you will probably have to use the auxiliaries *would*, *could*, and *might* because your arguments, objections, and counter arguments will be based on the condition that your proposal is accepted. For example, suppose that this is your proposal:

Class size should be limited to twelve students.

The condition "if class size were limited to twelve students" will be the basis of your entire composition, even if it is not written with each sentence. Note that in this conditional sentence, *were* is used with a singular subject (class size).

Example

(if class size were limited to twelve students) The teachers would be able to spend more time with each student. In addition, (if the class size were limited to twelve students) the students might get to know each other better. Finally, (if the class size were limited to twelve students) students could practice speaking more.

1 Read the following paragraph. Complete it by circling the correct modal auxiliary. Remember to use *would*, *could*, or *might* when there is a condition that is not presently true or real.

I believe that students in our class should be fined for speaking their native language during class time. This (will / would) [1] have several benefits. First of all, students (will / would) [2] learn to rely on English more. Second, students who don't speak the same native language (might / can) [3] get to know each other better. Third, students (will / would) [4] be more likely to tell the teacher when they are having problems. Finally, we (can / could) [5] use the money from the fines to have a party at the end of the semester.

Using Linking Expressions and Transition Words for Listing Ideas

Much of your essay will consist of lists. There will be a list of arguments in favor of your proposal, a list of possible objections, and a list of counter arguments. Since there are so many places where you will list ideas, it is important to use several different linking expressions and transition words. You can use these expressions at the beginning of each new paragraph and within the paragraphs.

Suppose that the first idea in your essay is the following: A day-care center would benefit the community by making it possible for mothers of young children to attend class. Here are some of the most common ways to add ideas to your composition using linking expressions.

Linking Expressions	**Examples of Additional Ideas**
also	It would *also* benefit the school . . .
another + noun	*Another* benefit would be that . . .
at the same time	*At the same time*, teachers would benefit.
Besides + noun or noun phrase	*Besides* benefiting the community, it would benefit the school. (*Besides* this, it would benefit the school.)
furthermore	*Furthermore*, the school would benefit.
in addition	*In addition*, the school would benefit.
moreover	*Moreover*, the school would benefit.
similarly	*Similarly*, it would benefit the school.

Here are some common transition words for listing ideas in order.

Transition Words	**Examples**
first (of all)	*First of all*, mothers of young children would be able to attend classes.
second	*Second*, school staff members would be able to use the center.
finally	*Finally*, the school would also receive many benefits from this type of program.

2 Complete the following paragraph with transition words and linking expressions; choose from those given in this section. Add punctuation where necessary.

There are several ways that the community would benefit from the establishment of a day-care center. __First of all__ (1) it would give non-English speakers a chance to go to school to learn English, and they would become more integrated into the life of the community. __________ (2) improving community relations, a day-care center would help non-English-speaking parents raise their standard of living because, if they learned English, they could get better jobs. __________ (3) the parents would be able to help their children with their schoolwork and communicate with their teachers. __________ (4) a day-care center would give non-English-speaking children and English-speaking children a chance to get to know each other. __________ (5) all parents (not just non-English speakers) would have a place to leave their children while they work.

Using Connecting Words and Transitions for Contrasting Ideas and Showing Cause and Result: Review

In your second-to-last paragraph, you will list possible objections and then counter them. To do this, you will need to review some of the connecting words and transitions you have already learned.

Connecting Words and Transitions for Contrasting Ideas

although even though nevertheless but however while

Connecting Words and Transitions for Showing Cause and Result

as a result consequently so because since therefore

3 Complete the following paragraph by circling the correct connecting words or transitions.

Several objections to a day-care center may be raised. First of all, some people may say that it is impossible ((because) / although) (1) it would be difficult to organize. (However / Therefore) (2), there are several students and staff members

who have day-care experience and are willing to set it up. Another objection might be that it would be expensive (while / so) the school would have to raise
3
tuition. (Consequently / But) this is not necessarily true. (Since / Although)
4 5
there would be some initial expense, it can be kept to a minimum by having participants donate used toys and books and pay a small enrollment fee.

Writing a Concluding Paragraph

4 Read this concluding paragraph and then answer the following questions about it.

In conclusion, because of the benefits to both the school and the community, the advantages of a day-care center clearly outweigh the disadvantages; therefore, I hope that the school administration will consider this proposal carefully.

---

1. What transition expression does the paragraph begin with? (Other possible concluding expressions are *in summary* and *to conclude.*)
2. Did the writer restate the ideas in different words?
3. How did the writer end the concluding paragraph? Did the writer use *will* or *would* after the verb *hope*?

Writing the First Draft

5 Write your essay using the outline you made. Remember to use transitions and connecting words in the essay. Write on every other line so you can revise your paragraphs easily.

PART 3 Edit and Revise

Editing Practice

1 Edit this paragraph for all errors, and rewrite it correctly. Then check it against the paragraph on page 183.

There is several way that the community would beneficial from establishment of day-care center. First, it would give non-English speakers a chance to go to school to learn English, and they will become more integrated into the life of the community. Besides improve community relations, a day-care center will help non-English-speaking parents raise their standard of living because, if they learned English, they can get better jobs. Also, parent would be able to help their children with their schoolwork and communicate with their teachers. Moreover, a day-care center gives non-English-speaking children and English-speaking children a chance to get to know one another. Finally, all parents (not just non-English speakers) would have a place to leave its child while they work.

Editing Your Writing

2 Edit your essay using the following checklist. First, check your essay for content, organization, cohesion, and style, using items 1, 2, and 3 in the checklist. Then edit it for grammar and form, using items 4 and 5.

Editing Checklist

1. Content
   a. Did you state the problem correctly?
   b. Did you give reasons for your proposal?
2. Organization
   a. Are your arguments appropriate for your audience?
   b. Did you counter any possible objections?
3. Cohesion and Style
   a. Did you use transition words for contrasting ideas correctly?
   b. Did you use transition words for enumerating ideas correctly?
4. Grammar
   Did you use the conditional mood correctly?
5. Form
   a. Did you use correct paragraph format? (indentation, division of words between syllables, margins)
   b. Did you use correct punctuation? (capitalization, commas, periods)
   c. Did you check the spelling of the words you are not sure of?

Peer Editing

3 Exchange papers with a classmate and edit each other's essays. Circle or underline in pencil any words, phrases, or sentences that you don't understand or that you think need to be corrected. Then return your essays. Discuss any questions you have with your partner.

Writing the Second Draft

4 After you edit your essay, rewrite it neatly, using correct form.

PART 4

A Step Beyond

Expansion Activities

1 Present your essay to the class as a speech. First, write the main ideas and important phrases on note cards. Then, on your own, practice giving the speech. Speak slowly and stress important words. Pause between phrases. Get to know the speech so that you can look at the audience while you speak.

2 Look at the paragraph on page 181 on fining students for speaking their native language during class time. You are going to expand this paragraph into a six-paragraph essay. Work in small groups. Begin by outlining the four arguments the author presents. Then suggest details and examples to further develop each of the four arguments. Finally, write out the new essay, including introductory and concluding paragraphs.

3 Working on your own, write a four- to six-paragraph essay taking the opposite side of the English-only issue presented in Activity 2. (Or take the opposite side of your own essay that you wrote for this chapter.)

4 Find articles in newspapers and magazines on both sides of a controversial topic. (You can look for articles in English in a library or on the Internet. If you cannot find articles in English, read some in your native language.) Discuss the articles with your classmates. What are the opposing viewpoints? What is your opinion?

Journal Writing

5 Write for fifteen minutes about one or both of the following topics.

1. Write about the most important issue or problem facing you in your life at this moment.
2. Write on a possible solution to the problem or issue you described in the preceding activity.

6 Since this is the end of the course, you should now do a self-evaluation. Look at the comments your teacher has given you throughout the course and answer these questions.

1. How have you improved?
2. What are your strong points?
3. What are your weak points?
4. What should you be especially careful of when you revise?
5. What should you be especially careful of when you edit?
6. How do you feel about writing in English now?

Video Activities: Justice and Racism

Before You Watch. Discuss the meanings of the following words in a group. Check the meanings in a dictionary if necessary.

Justice Jury Defendant Guilty Verdict Convict (verb) Testimony

Watch. Discuss the following questions in a group.

1. At the beginning of the video, the announcer says, "Justice is supposed to be blind, including color blind, but is it?" What is the answer to this question, according to the video?
2. Who is more racist, judges or juries? Why?
3. According to Judge Danielson, what is the solution to the problem of racism in the justice system?

Watch Again. Below are incomplete statements from the video. Try to guess the missing words. Then watch the video again and check your answers.

a. "Because racism still exists in our society, we see it in our court __________________."

b. "__________________ may say they're impartial, but sometimes they make comments to other __________________ about the defendant."

c. "Each judge knows that he or she has an ethical __________________ to deal with (racism) when it occurs in the courtroom."

d. "Racism is going to be __________________ with us right on into the millennium, even in our criminal justice system."

After You Watch. In the video clip, Judge Danielson says the solution to racism is "knowledge, awareness, and education. Before you can solve a problem, it has to be in your mind." Do you agree with the judge? What, in your opinion, is the solution to the problem of racism? Write your opinion. Then share what you wrote with your classmates.

Appendices

Appendix 1

Spelling Rules for Adding Endings

Endings That Begin with Vowels (*-ed, -ing, -er, -est*)

1. For words ending in a silent *e,* drop the *e* and add the ending.

   like → lik**ed** mak → mak**ing** safe → saf**er** fine → fin**est**

2. For one-syllable words ending in a single vowel and a single consonant, double the final consonant.

   bat → bat**ted** **run** → run**ning** **fat** → fat**ter** **hot** → hot**test**

3. Don't double the final consonant when the word has two final consonants or two vowels before a final consonant.

   pi**ck** → pick**ed** si**ng** → sing**ing** cl**ean** → clean**er** c**oo**l → cool**est**

4. For words of two or more syllables that end in a single vowel and a single consonant, double the final consonant if the word is accented on the final syllable.

   reférr → refer**red** begín → begin**ning**

5. For words of two or more syllables that end in a single vowel and a single consonant, make no change if the word isn't accented on the final syllable.

   trável → travel**ed** fócus → focus**ed**

6. For words ending in a consonant and *y,* change the *y* to *i* and add the ending unless the ending begins with *i.*

   study → stud**ied** dirty → dirt**ier** sunny → sunn**iest**

   study → study**ing** hurry → hurry**ing**

7. For words ending in a vowel and *y,* make no change before adding the ending.

   pl**ay** → play**ed** st**ay** → stay**ing**

Endings That Begin with Consonants (*-ly, -ment*)

1. For words ending in a silent *e,* make no change when adding endings that begin with consonants.

   fine → fine**ly** state → state**ment**

2. For words ending in a consonant and *y,* change the *y* to *i* before adding the ending.

   hap**py** → happ**ily** mer**ry** → merr**iment**

Adding a Final *s* to Nouns and Verbs

1. Generally, add the *s* without making changes.

   sit → sit**s** dance → dance**s** play → play**s** book → book**s**

2. If a word ends in a consonant and *y*, change the *y* to *i* and add *es*.

   mar**ry** → mar**ries** stu**dy** → stu**dies** cher**ry** → cher**ries**

3. If a word ends in *ch, s, sh, x,* or *z,* add *es*.

   chur**ch** → church**es** ca**sh** → cash**es** fi**zz** → fizz**es**

   bo**ss** → boss**es** mi**x** → mix**es**

4. For words ending in *o*, sometimes add *es* and sometimes add *s*.

   tomat**o** → tomato**es** potat**o** → potato**es**

   pian**o** → piano**s** radi**o** → radio**s**

5. For words ending in *f* or *fe*, generally drop the *f* or *fe* and add *ves*.

   kni**fe** → kni**ves** wi**fe** → wi**ves** li**fe** → li**ves** loa**f** → loa**ves**

   Exceptions: sa**fe** → safe**s** pu**ff** → puff**s** roo**f** → roof**s**

Appendix 2

Capitalization Rules

First Words

1. Capitalize the first word of every sentence.

   They live in Rome. **W**ho is it?

2. Capitalize the first word of a quotation.

   He said, "**M**y name is Paul." Jenny asked, "**W**hen is the party?"

Personal Names

1. Capitalize the names of people including initials and titles of address.

   Mrs. **J**ones **M**ohandas **G**andhi **J**ohn **F.** **K**ennedy

2. Capitalize family words if they appear alone or followed by a name.

   Let's go, **D**ad. Where's **G**randma? She's at **A**unt Lucy's.

3. Don't capitalize family words with a possessive pronoun or article.

   my **u**ncle her **m**other our **g**randparents an **a**unt

4. Capitalize the pronoun *I*.

   I have a book. She's bigger than **I** am.

5. Capitalize names of God.

   God **A**llah **J**esus **C**hrist

6. Capitalize the names of nationalities, races, peoples, and religions.

   Japanese **A**rab **A**sian **C**hicano **M**uslim

7. Generally, don't capitalize occupations.

   I am a **s**ecretary. She wants to be a **l**awyer.

Place Names

1. Capitalize the names of countries, states, provinces, and cities.

   Mexico **N**ew **Y**ork **O**ntario **T**okyo

2. Capitalize the names of oceans, lakes, rivers, islands, and mountains.

   the **A**tlantic **O**cean **L**ake **C**omo the **A**mazon **B**elle **I**sle **M**t. **E**verest

3. Capitalize the names of geographical areas.

   the **S**outh the **E**ast **C**oast **A**sia **A**ntarctica

4. Don't capitalize directions if they aren't names of geographical areas.

   He lives **e**ast of Toronto. They traveled **s**outhwest.

5. Capitalize names of schools, parks, buildings, and streets.

   the **U**niversity of **G**eorgia **C**entral **P**ark the **S**ears **B**uilding **O**xford **R**oad

Time Words

1. Capitalize names of days and months.

   Monday **F**riday **J**anuary **M**arch

2. Capitalize names of holidays and historical events.

   Christmas **N**ew **Y**ear's **D**ay **I**ndependence **D**ay **W**orld **W**ar II

3. Don't capitalize names of seasons.

   spring **s**ummer **f**all **w**inter

Titles

1. Capitalize the first word and all important words of titles of books, magazines, newspapers, and articles.

   Interactions *Newsweek* *The New York Times* "**R**ock **M**usic **T**oday"

2. Capitalize the first word and all important words of names of movies, plays, radio programs, and television programs.

   The African Queen *The Tempest* "**N**ews **R**oundup" "**F**ame"

3. Don't capitalize articles (*a, an, the*), conjunctions (*but, and, or*), and short prepositions (*of, with, in, on, for*) unless they are the first word of a title.

   *The Life **of** Thomas Edison* *War **and** Peace* *Death **of a** Salesman*

Names of Organizations

1. Capitalize the names of organizations, government groups, and businesses.

   International **S**tudent **A**ssociation the **S**enate **G**estetner

2. Capitalize trade names, but do not capitalize the names of the product.

   IBM computer **T**oyota hatchback **K**ellogg's cereal

Other

1. Capitalize the names of languages

   Spanish **T**hai **F**rench **J**apanese

2. Don't capitalize school subjects unless they are the names of languages or are followed by a number.

   geometry **m**usic **E**nglish **A**rabic **B**iology 306

Appendix 3

Punctuation Rules

Period

1. Use a period after a statement or command.

   We are studying English. Open your books to Chapter 3.

2. Use a period after most abbreviations.

   Mr. Ms. Dr. Ave. etc. U.S.

   Exceptions: UN NATO IBM AIDS

3. Use a period after initials.

   H. G. Wells Dr. H. R. Hammond

Question Mark

1. Use a question mark after (not before) questions.

   Where are you going? Is he here yet?

2. In a direct quotation, the question mark goes before the quotation marks.

   He asked, "What's your name?"

Exclamation Point

Use an exclamation point after exclamatory sentences or phrases.

I won the lottery! Be quiet! Wow!

Comma

1. Use a comma before a conjunction (*and, or, so, but*) that separates two independent clauses.

   She wanted to go to work, so she decided to take an English course.

   He wasn't happy in that apartment, but he didn't have the money to move.

2. Don't use a comma before a conjunction that separates two phrases that aren't complete sentences.

   She worked in the library and studied at night.

   Do you want to go to a movie or stay home?

3. Use a comma before an introductory clause or phrase (generally if it is five or more words long).

   After a beautiful wedding ceremony, they had a reception in her mother's home.

   If you want to write well, you should practice writing almost every night.

4. Use a comma to separate interrupting expressions from the rest of a sentence.

   Do you know, by the way, what time dinner is?

   Many of the students, I found out, stayed on campus during the summer.

5. Use a comma after transitional expressions.

   In addition, he stole all her jewelry.

   However, he left the TV.

   Common transitional expressions are:

therefore	in addition	in fact	on the other hand
consequently	moreover	similarly	for example
for this reason	furthermore	however	for instance
also	besides	nevertheless	

6. Use a comma to separate names of people in direct address from the rest of a sentence.

   Jane, have you seen Paul?

   We aren't sure, Mrs. Shapiro, where he is.

7. Use a comma after *yes* and *no* in answers.

   Yes, he was here a minute ago.

   No, I haven't.

8. Use a comma to separate items in a series.

   We have coffee, tea, and milk.

   He looked in the refrigerator, on the shelves, and in the cupboard.

9. Use a comma to separate an appositive from the rest of a sentence.

   Mrs. Sampson, his English teacher, gave him a good recommendation.

   Would you like to try a taco, a delicious Mexican food?

10. If a date or address has two or more parts, use a comma after each part.

    I was born on June 5, 1968.

    The house at 230 Seventh Street, Miami, Florida, is for sale.

11. Use a comma to separate contrasting information from the rest of the sentence.

    It wasn't Maria, but Parvin, who was absent.

    Bring your writing book, not your reading book.

12. Use a comma to separate quotations from the rest of a sentence.

    He asked, "What are we going to do?"

    "I'm working downtown," he said.

13. Use a comma to separate two or more adjectives that each modify the noun alone.

    She was an intelligent, beautiful actress. (*intelligent* and *beautiful* actress)

    Eat those delicious green beans. (*delicious* modifies *green beans*)

14. Use a comma to separate nonrestrictive clauses from the rest of a sentence. A nonrestrictive clause gives more information about the noun it describes, but it isn't needed to identify the noun. Clauses after proper names are nonrestrictive and require commas.

    It's a Wonderful Life, which is often on television at Christmastime, is my favorite movie.

    James Stewart, who plays a man thinking of killing himself, is the star of *It's a Wonderful Life*.

Quotation Marks

1. Use quotation marks at the beginning and end of exact quotations. Other punctuation marks go before the end quotation marks.

   He said, "I'm going to Montreal."

   "How are you?" he asked.

2. Use quotation marks before and after titles of stories, articles, songs, and television programs. Periods and commas go before the final quotation marks, while question marks and exclamation points normally go after them.

   Do you like to watch "Dallas" on television?

   My favorite song is "Let It Be."

   Do you like the story "Gift of the Magi"?

Apostrophes

1. Use apostrophes in contractions.

   don't   it's   we've   they're

2. Use an apostrophe to make possessive nouns.

Singular:	Jerry's	my boss's
Plural:	the children's	the Smiths'

Underlining

Underline the titles of books, magazines, newspapers, plays, and movies.

I am reading <u>One Hundred Years of Solitude</u>.

Did you like the movie <u>The Wizard of Oz</u>?

Appendix 4

A List of Noncount Nouns

Food

bread, butter, cheese, chicken,* chocolate,* coffee,* cream, fish,* flour, fruit,* ice cream,* juice,* meat, milk,* rice, salt, spaghetti, sugar, tea

Natural Phenomena

Weather words: rain, snow,* sunshine, thunder, wind*

Gases: air, hydrogen, nitrogen, oxygen

Minerals: copper, gold, iron, silver, steel

Materials: dirt, dust, earth, grass, ice, land,* oil, sand, water*

Activities and Sports

baseball,* chess, dance,* skating, soccer, tennis

Emotions and Qualities†

ambition, anger, courage, fear, freedom, happiness, hatred, honesty, justice, loneliness, love, joy, pride

Social Issues†

abortion, crime, democracy, divorce, hunger, nuclear power, peace, pollution, poverty

Mass Nouns (Composed of Dissimilar Items)

change, clothing, fruit, equipment, furniture, jewelry, luggage, mail, machinery, makeup, medicine, money, noise, scenery, technology, transportation, vocabulary

---

* These nouns are sometimes count and sometimes noncount. They are noncount when they refer to the item in general. They are count when they refer to a particular item.

I like coffee and tea.

Please give me one coffee and two teas.

† Most emotions, qualities, and social issues can function as count nouns: *a strong ambition, a deep hatred, a terrible crime.*

Subjects

art,* economics, history,* humanities, physics

Miscellaneous

advice, business,* fun, glass,* homework, knowledge,* information, insurance, life, nature,* news, paint,* publicity, reality,* research, sleep, time,* traffic, trouble, tuition, work*

Appendix 5

Subordinating Conjunctions

Subordinating conjunctions can show relationships of *time, reason, contrast,* and *purpose.*

1. Time: *when, whenever, if*
2. Reason: *because, since*
3. Contrast: *although, even though, though*
4. Purpose: *so that*

Appendix 6

Transitions

Transitions are words or phrases that join two related ideas. Here is a list of the most common transitions.

1. Giving examples: *for example, for instance*
2. Adding emphasis: *in fact, of course*
3. Adding information: *in addition, furthermore, moreover, besides*
4. Making comparisons: *similarly, likewise*
5. Showing contrast: *however, nevertheless, in contrast, on the contrary, on one hand/on the other hand*
6. Giving reasons or results: *therefore, as a result, as a consequence, for this (that) reason*
7. Giving sequences: *now, then, first (second, etc.), earlier, later, meanwhile, finally*

Chapter 1 — Feedback Sheet

Student Name ______________________________ Date ____________

Personal Reaction

____

____

____

____

Chapter Checklist	**Good**	**Needs Work**
1. Content		
a. Did you include everything that you wanted to say?	❑	❑
b. Did you give a reason for each opinion?	❑	❑
2. Organization		
a. Does your topic sentence give the main idea of your paragraph?	❑	❑
b. Did you organize your ideas from most important to least important?	❑	❑
3. Cohesion and Style		
a. Did you use transition words and connectors?	❑	❑
b. Did you use adverbs of frequency and quantifiers?	❑	❑
4. Grammar		
a. Did you use present tense verbs?	❑	❑
b. Did you use adverbs of frequency and quantifiers?		
5. Form		
a. Did you use correct paragraph format (indentation, division of words between syllables, margins)?	❑	❑
b. Did you use correct punctuation (capitalization, commas, periods)?	❑	❑
c. Did you check the spelling of words you were not sure of?	❑	❑

Other Comments

____

____

____

____

Chapter 2 — Feedback Sheet

Student Name ______________________________ Date ______________

Personal Reaction

____

____

____

____

Chapter Checklist	Good	Needs Work
1. Content		
a. Did you add enough descriptive details?	❑	❑
b. Did you use a variety of adjectives?	❑	❑
2. Organization		
a. Is your topic sentence the main idea of your paragraph?	❑	❑
b. Do all the details develop the topic sentence?	❑	❑
c. Did you include a concluding sentence?	❑	❑
3. Cohesion and Style		
a. Have you given reasons for your feelings?	❑	❑
b. Have you varied word order of your sentences?	❑	❑
4. Grammar		
a. Did you avoid run-on sentences?	❑	❑
b. Did you use correct verb forms?	❑	❑
5. Form		
a. Did you use correct paragraph format (indentation, division of words between syllables, margins)?	❑	❑
b. Did you use correct punctuation (capitalization, commas, periods)?	❑	❑
c. Did you check the spelling of words you were not sure of?	❑	❑

Other Comments

____

____

____

____

Chapter 3 **Feedback Sheet**

Student Name ______________________________ Date ______________

Personal Reaction

____

____

____

____

Chapter Checklist	**Good**	**Needs Work**
1. Content		
a. Did you state your opinion clearly?	❏	❏
b. Did you support your opinion with reasons?	❏	❏
c. Did you support your reasons with examples and/or predictions?	❏	❏
d. Did you avoid faulty reasoning?	❏	❏
2. Organization		
a. Did you write an opening sentence that told what article you are responding to and gave your opinion?	❏	❏
b. Did you write a concluding sentence?	❏	❏
3. Cohesion and Style		
a. Did you use transitions?	❏	❏
b. Did you state your opinions using appropriate modals?	❏	❏
c. Did you use a moderate or a strong style to express your opinions?	❏	❏
4. Grammar		
a. Did you use simple verb forms with modals?	❏	❏
b. Did you use present verb forms in *if* clauses and future verb forms in predictions?	❏	❏
c. Did you avoid run-on sentences?	❏	❏
5. Form		
a. Did you use correct paragraph format (indentation, margins, capitals at beginning of sentences?	❏	❏
b. Did you use correct spelling and syllabification?	❏	❏

Other Comments

____

____

____

____

Chapter 4 Feedback Sheet

Student Name ______________________________ Date ____________

Personal Reaction

____

____

____

____

Chapter Checklist	**Good**	**Needs Work**
1. Content		
a. Does your paragraph describe your best qualities?	❑	❑
b. Does it show that you can be successful in what you do?	❑	❑
c. Does it let the reader infer what your best qualities are?	❑	❑
2. Organization		
a. Do you have too many ideas for one paragraph? Should you divide your paragraph into two paragraphs?	❑	❑
b. Are there any ideas not relevant to the topic?	❑	❑
c. Is your topic sentence positive? Does it make the reader want to find out more about you?	❑	❑
d. Does each sentence add a new idea? Should you take out or combine repetitive sentences?	❑	❑
e. Does your concluding sentence tell something you've learned or something you hope for in the future?	❑	❑
3. Cohesion and Style		
a. Have you used verb tenses correctly?	❑	❑
b. Can you add demonstratives *(this, that, these, those)* and prepositional phrases with demonstratives to unify your paragraph?	❑	❑
4. Grammar		
a. Are your verb forms correct?	❑	❑
b. Have you used run-on sentences or sentence fragments?	❑	❑
c. Have you used plural and singular demonstratives correctly?	❑	❑
5. Form		
a. Is your capitalization correct?	❑	❑
b. Is your spelling of past participles correct?	❑	❑

Other Comments

____

____

____

Chapter 5 — Feedback Sheet

Student Name ______________________________ Date ____________

Personal Reaction

____
____
____
____

Chapter Checklist	**Good**	**Needs Work**
1. Content		
a. Is your story interesting?	❑	❑
b. Does the lesson (conclusion) fit the story you told?	❑	❑
c. Have you given enough information?	❑	❑
2. Organization		
a. Have you avoided unimportant details and digressions?	❑	❑
b. Have you used paragraph divisions to make the story clearer?	❑	❑
3. Cohesion and Style		
a. Have you used transition words correctly?	❑	❑
b. Are your sentences in logical order?	❑	❑
4. Grammar		
Have you used the past, present perfect, and past perfect tenses correctly?	❑	❑
5. Form		
a. Did you use correct paragraph format (indentation, division of words between syllables, margins)?	❑	❑
b. Did you use correct punctuation (capitalization, commas, periods)?	❑	❑
c. Did you check the spelling of the words you were not sure of?	❑	❑

Other Comments

____
____
____
____

Chapter 6 — Feedback Sheet

Student Name ______________________________ Date ______________

Personal Reaction

____

____

____

____

Chapter Checklist	**Good**	**Needs Work**
1. Content		
Does your paragraph give examples when necessary?	❑	❑
2. Organization		
Does your paragraph have a narrow-enough focus?	❑	❑
3. Cohesion and Style		
Have you used relative clauses correctly?	❑	❑
4. Grammar		
a. Have you used the correct part of speech for each word?	❑	❑
b. Have you used relative clauses correctly?	❑	❑
5. Form		
a. Have you used a capital letter to begin each sentence?	❑	❑
b. Have you used a period to end each sentence?	❑	❑
c. Have you punctuated relative clauses correctly?	❑	❑

Other Comments

____

____

____

____

Chapter 7 — Feedback Sheet

Student Name ______________________________ Date ______________

Personal Reaction

____

____

____

____

Chapter Checklist	**Good**	**Needs Work**
1. Content		
a. Is the information interesting?	❑	❑
b. Does the composition answer most of the reader's questions?	❑	❑
2. Organization		
a. Are paragraphs organized chronologically?	❑	❑
b. Does your first paragraph have a good topic sentence?	❑	❑
c. Does your last paragraph have a concluding sentence?	❑	❑
3. Cohesion and Style		
a. Are your gerund and infinitive constructions parallel?	❑	❑
b. Did you use *used to* too often?	❑	❑
4. Grammar		
a. Did you use *used to* and *would* correctly?	❑	❑
b. Did you use verbal adjectives correctly?	❑	❑
5. Form		
a. Did you use correct paragraph format (indentation, division of words between syllables, margins)?	❑	❑
b. Did you use correct punctuation (capitalization, commas, periods)?	❑	❑
c. Did you check the spelling of the words you were not sure of?	❑	❑

Other Comments

____

____

____

____

Chapter 8

Feedback Sheet

Student Name ______________________________ Date ____________

Personal Reaction

____

____

____

____

Chapter Checklist	Good	Needs Work
1. Content Does your composition list all the similarities and differences you think are important?	❏	❏
2. Organization a. Does the topic sentence mention both similarities and differences even though it focuses on one or the other?	❏	❏
b. Does one paragraph deal with differences and the other with similarities?	❏	❏
3. Cohesion and Style Have you used expressions as *both, neither, in contrast, on the other hand,* and *while?*	❏	❏
4. Grammar a. Have you used gerunds correctly?	❏	❏
b. Have you used comparatives and superlatives correctly?	❏	❏
5. Form a. Have you used a capital letter to begin each sentence?	❏	❏
b. Have you used a period to end each sentence?	❏	❏

Other Comments

____

____

____

____

Chapter 9 — Feedback Sheet

Student Name ______________________________ Date ______________

Personal Reaction

____

____

____

____

Chapter Checklist	**Good**	**Needs Work**
1. Content		
a. Is your information accurate?	❑	❑
b. Have you made interesting comparisons?	❑	❑
2. Organization		
Is the information organized logically?	❑	❑
3. Cohesion and Style		
a. Did you vary the word order in some sentences, using *with* + noun phrase, *because* and *because of?*	❑	❑
b. Did you use *unlike* + noun phrase to show contrast?	❑	❑
4. Grammar		
a. Did you use the passive voice correctly?	❑	❑
b. Did you use correct tenses?	❑	❑
5. Form		
a. Did you use correct paragraph format (indentation, division of words between syllables, margins)?	❑	❑
b. Did you use correct punctuation (capitalization, commas, periods)?	❑	❑
c. Did you check the spelling of the words you were not sure of?	❑	❑

Other Comments

____

____

____

____

Chapter 10 — Feedback Sheet

Student Name ______________________________ Date ______________

Personal Reaction

____

____

____

____

Chapter Checklist	**Good**	**Needs Work**
1. Content		
a. Did you support your opinion with good reasons?	❑	❑
b. Is your composition interesting?	❑	❑
2. Organization		
a. Do you have an introduction, supporting paragraphs, and a conclusion?	❑	❑
b. Is your focus clear?	❑	❑
3. Cohesion and Style		
a. Did you introduce your examples with transitions?	❑	❑
b. Did you use quotations?	❑	❑
4. Grammar		
a. Did you use indefinite forms correctly?	❑	❑
b. Did you use generalizations correctly?	❑	❑
5. Form		
a. Did you use correct paragraph format (indentation, division of words between syllables, margins)?	❑	❑
b. Did you use correct punctuation (capitalization, commas, periods)?	❑	❑
c. Did you check the spelling of the words you were not sure of?	❑	❑

Other Comments

____

____

____

____

Chapter 11 **Feedback Sheet**

Student Name ______________________________ Date ____________

Personal Reaction

____

____

____

____

Chapter Checklist	**Good**	**Needs Work**
1. Content		
a. Is your article interesting?	❑	❑
b. Does it provide enough detail?	❑	❑
2. Organization		
a. Does your article answer the questions Who? What? Where? When? Why?	❑	❑
b. Did you have an appropriate title?	❑	❑
c. Did you include facts and not personal opinions?	❑	❑
3. Cohesion and Style		
a. Did you use restrictive relative clauses correctly?	❑	❑
b. Did you use nonrestrictive relative clauses correctly?	❑	❑
4. Grammar		
a. Did you punctuate relative clauses correctly?	❑	❑
b. Did you use correct verb tenses?	❑	❑
5. Form		
a. Did you use correct paragraph format (indentations, division of words between syllables, margins)?	❑	❑
b. Did you use correct punctuation (capitalization, commas, periods)?	❑	❑
c. Did you check the spelling of the words you were not sure of?	❑	❑

Other Comments

____

____

____

____

Chapter 12 — Feedback Sheet

Student Name ______________________________ Date ____________

Personal Reaction

____

____

____

____

Chapter Checklist	**Good**	**Needs Work**
1. Content		
a. Did you state the problem clearly?	❑	❑
b. Did you give reasons for your proposal?	❑	❑
2. Organization		
a. Are your arguments appropriate for your audience?	❑	❑
b. Did you counter any possible objections?	❑	❑
3. Cohesion and Style		
a. Did you use the transition words for contrasting ideas correctly?	❑	❑
b. Did you use transition words for enumerating ideas correctly?	❑	❑
4. Grammar		
Did you use the conditional mood correctly?	❑	❑
5. Form		
a. Did you use correct paragraph format (indentation, division of words between syllables, margins)?	❑	❑
b. Did you use correct punctuation (capitalization, commas, periods)?	❑	❑
c. Did you check the spelling of the words you were not sure of?	❑	❑

Other Comments

____

____

____

____